# Chicago Tribune

# THE '85 BEARS STILL CHICAGO'S TEAM

TRIUMPH
BOOKS
CHICAGO

**WILLIE? HE WILL:** An uncomfortable Willie Gault hauls in a pass against New England's Ronnie Lippett for one of Gault's four Super Bowl catches.

**Chicago Tribune**

Copyright ©2005 by The Chicago Tribune.
All rights reserved.

Library of Congress Control Number:
2005930472

This book is available in quantity at special
discounts for your group or organization.
For further information, contact:

Triumph Books
542 S. Dearborn St.
Suite 750
Chicago, IL 60605
Phone: (312) 939-3330
Fax: (312) 663-3557

Printed in the United States of America
ISBN-13: 978-1-57243-792-0
ISBN-10: 1-57243-792-8

**FLATTENED:**
Wilber Marshall
sends Lions quarter-
back Joe Ferguson
to the turf in the
regular-season finale.

**SHOT DOWN:**
Jim McMahon
is thwarted in his
airborne attempt
to score against the
Patriots in Game 2.

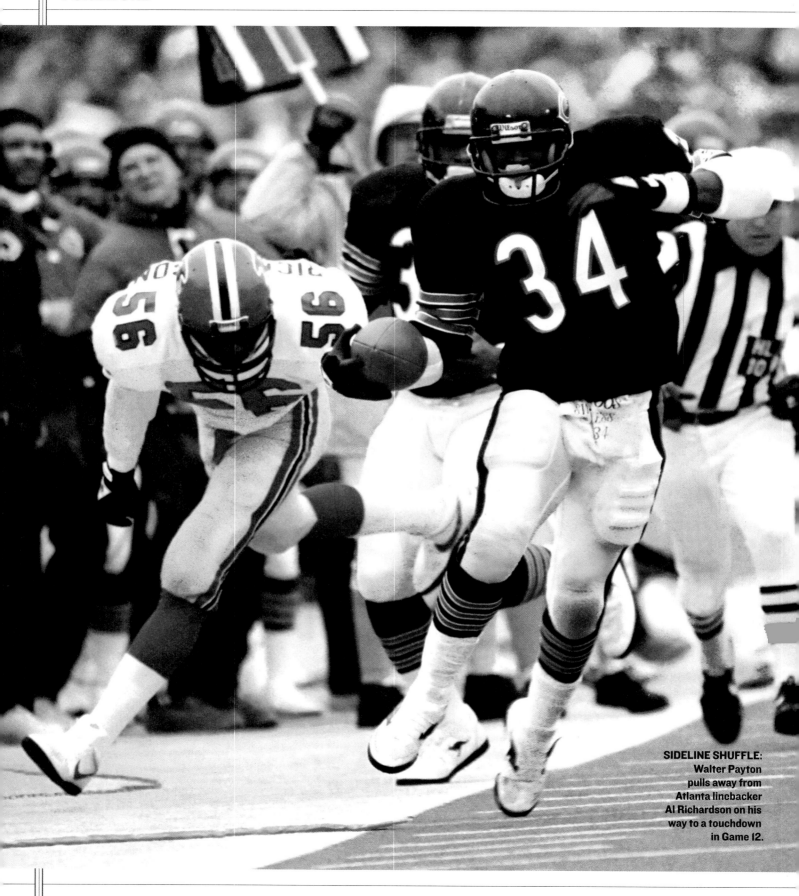

**SIDELINE SHUFFLE:**
Walter Payton
pulls away from
Atlanta linebacker
Al Richardson on his
way to a touchdown
in Game 12.

*By* CONNIE PAYTON

# Living the spirit of Sweetness

**A**s a football player, my husband was revered for his all-around ability and his effort. He could run, catch, pass, kick and block. He did it all with flair and determination, and he never gave anything but his best.

To this day, Mike Ditka says Walter was "the best I have ever seen."

Six years since his passing and 20 years since he played for the Super Bowl champion Bears, my memories of Walter as a husband, father and football player remain indelibly etched in my mind.

Walter loved his family, he loved the fans and he loved his teammates. He would be the first in line to laugh and joke with them if he were alive today.

Walter passed away on Nov. 1, 1999, following an illness brought on by a liver ailment. He was 45. Hardly a day goes by that I don't fulfill a speaking engagement or a dedication ceremony in his name. The number of lives Walter touched is just amazing.

I have kept very busy the last six years, but it has been nice to be involved in things where you feel you are making a difference. Being able to speak about the importance of the organ-donor program has been great. And starting a cancer fund and continuing to run the Walter & Connie Payton Foundation has been very gratifying.

I have my good days and I have some bad days, but for the most part I just try to get up every day and make it a good day. Not a day goes by that I don't think of Walter. Just looking at the kids … Jarrett has more of his personality and Brittney his features. You just see Walter's presence all the time.

If you had asked him about his fondest memories of playing football with the Bears all those years, Walter would not mention all his individual records. He would not talk about the Hall of Fame accolades after his career. He would talk about the people he met, the teammates he loved, the practical jokes he pulled and the less fortunate people he was able to help along the way because of his position as a professional athlete.

As a football player, a businessman and a person, Walter never quit trying to reach for that extra yard, that extra edge to help the team, or to help another person less fortunate than himself.

He repeatedly would say how he felt less than physically superior as a young football player, but that hard work and a fear of failure drove him to maximize his abilities.

"You can't set limits for yourself," he would say. "You have to constantly push yourself. No matter what you do for a living, you know when you're doing your best or you're just mailing it in. When I'm playing football, I want to leave it all out there on the field like it's the last game of my life."

As we celebrate the 20th anniversary of the Bears' Super Bowl championship, let's all continue to keep Walter's spirit and memory alive.

*Connie Payton*

# Contents

**FIELD OF DREAMS:**
Fans' hopes for a
Super Bowl come a
step closer as the
Bears shut out the
Giants in the
NFC semifinal at
Soldier Field.

*By* DON PIERSON

# City in a mirror: Grit and heart

**T**hey did more than win; they dominated.

They did more than play; they entertained.

They were more than fun; they were hilarious.

The 1985 Bears were more than memorable; they were unforgettable.

They were controversial yet conservative, innovative yet old-fashioned, feared yet loved, arrogant yet endearing. And that was just Da Coach, Mike Ditka.

They not only fought off every foe except the Miami Dolphins, they fought with each other over commercials, over a table of hats minutes after their Super Bowl victory, over who should be playing, over who should be scoring in a Super Bowl so lopsided there was nothing else to complain about.

George Halas didn't live to see them win, but he helped set it up, hiring Ditka yet forcing him to keep defensive coordinator Buddy Ryan, fomenting the kind of creative tension Halas always encouraged and enjoyed.

It was coach against quarterback, coach against coach, defensive tackle against defensive tackle, offense against defense.

It also was all for one and one for all. And one and done.

They will kick themselves to their graves over winning only one NFL championship, squandering opportunity and talent. Yet even that aching void adds to the aura of the greatest single season the Bears—and quite possibly the NFL—ever had.

Because no other Bears team has come close to winning since, the '85 Bears' popularity grows rather than diminishes. They took marketing to new levels and continue to sell themselves today as a corporation, The 1985 World Champions XX, Inc.

Fans who were in their 20s then bask in the nostalgia and tell their children. Fans who were in their 40s are resigned to never seeing their like.

As they travel the happy road from history to legend, heading toward myth, it is time to pause and review some reasons the Bears of '85 gripped the imagination and cling to it still today.

## I. IT'S A FOOTBALL TOWN

The Bears have won only two titles since the '40s, when they won four. In some towns, such unrequited love is grounds for divorce. In Chicago, such frequent success is cause for celebration. The Bears have an insurmountable lead on the Cubs and White Sox, for example.

The Bulls, relative newcomers, have Michael Jordan and six titles. The Bears have

**OVERSIZED LOAD:**
Jay Hilgenberg piles
aboard a motor
scooter piloted by
a teammate at
training camp in
Platteville, Wis.

Red Grange and Bronko Nagurski and Sid Luckman and Bulldog Turner and Bill George and Dick Butkus and Gale Sayers and Walter Payton and Mike Singletary and Dan Hampton and nine titles.

Carl Sandburg's City of the Big Shoulders and Hog Butcher for the World conjures up images of middle linebackers and running backs, not shortstops and shooting guards.

So what if the Bears win only every 20 years or so? Everything is relative. When it happens, it is good and proper to preserve and savor every moment. Heck, one of the players on the 1963 champions, Maury Youmans, recently wrote a book about that year.

## 2. DOMINANCE

When the Bears fell behind the New England Patriots 3-0 in Super Bowl XX, a shudder went down the backs of Chicago sports fans who braced for the worst despite so much evidence of supremacy.

The Bears were so good that Los Angeles Rams coach John Robinson later confided that the NFC championship game against the Bears had been the only time he'd ever entered a game knowing he had no chance.

Payton was football's all-time leading rusher and still very much a force in his 11th season. The offensive line was outstanding, with Jim Covert, Mark Bortz, Jay Hilgenberg, Tom Thayer and Keith Van Horne all in their prime. Quarterback Jim McMahon knew at least as much offense as some of the coaches and was the brash leader of the seventh-ranked attack in the league.

Yet the offense paled compared with the defense. Most teams try to mask weaknesses; the Bears exploited strengths. Extremely talented from front to back, the defense was without a significant flaw at any position. But the "46" scheme of coordinator Buddy Ryan made the defense downright dangerous. It was overkill. The defense became like a SWAT team using an illegal weapon.

Later, Richie Petitbon, who starred on the 1963 championship team, would wonder how Ryan got away with what was essentially an unsound strategy. Receivers would be running free, but quarterbacks would be running for their lives, unable to get rid of the ball. Eventually, offenses caught up by using shorter drops and quicker passes. But in 1985, the Bears' jailbreak aggressiveness was a scourge without an antidote.

There have been disputed championships, fluke championships, close championships and plenty of championship teams that left room for argument. The '85 Bears left no doubt and few prisoners.

Falling one game short of perfection—the lone what-if on the résumé—failed to shake

**FREEZE FRAME:** William Perry is the center of attention during introductions at Texas Stadium before the Bears blanked the Cowboys 44-0.

**DEFENSIVE POSTURE:** Richard Dent strips Giants quarterback Phil Simms of the ball during the Bears' NFC semifinal victory. Defensive tackle Steve McMichael inhales an oxygen treat during the season and coordinator Buddy Ryan (right) and aide Jeff Fisher look over the defense.

their confidence an iota. The day after that Monday night loss in Miami on Dec. 2—a full eight weeks before the Super Bowl—they videotaped "The Super Bowl Shuffle," ensuring their immortality win or lose the biggest game of their lives.

The primitive production convinced generations to come that the Bears must have been good football players, because they weren't going to make a living rapping or dancing.

### 3. DITKA

The Bears have had three coaches since Ditka, and not one of them has thrown bubble gum at a fan or asked anybody, "What's your IQ, buddy?"

None of them had a face like a grizzly Bear, either, the very embodiment of one of the league's original and most familiar logos. None of them performs regularly on national television, appears in a movie playing himself, owns a restaurant or stares out from the labels of mustard jars on grocery shelves.

None of the Bears' coaches since Ditka has won consistently, either, which provides a convenient main attraction to the sideshow. Ditka did and is still doing what no other Bears coaches have done, making it impossible for 1985 to fade into the background.

At his first team meeting, Ditka told his players they would win a Super Bowl. They hadn't heard such talk before, and nobody has heard the last of it since.

### 4. THE CHARACTERS

Ditka only led the parade of personalities, providing the template for how to have fun and make money while playing football. When Commissioner Pete Rozelle routinely fined McMahon for displaying a series of names and ads on his headband, Rozelle also confided to Ditka that he was a fan of the team that revived fun.

William "The Refrigerator" Perry was only a rookie, and at a time when 300-pounders were still novelties, the Fridge made a

belly-whopping splash. He became the Falstaff of a team that was already full of merriment.

Ryan was not cut out to work in Ditka's shadow, so the team in effect had two head coaches, as pictures of both being carried off the Super Bowl field will attest. Ryan and Ditka seemed to compete for outrageous quotes, serving as examples to players who learned to love the microphones.

Ditka, Hampton, Thayer, Covert, Van Horne, Steve McMichael, Dave Duerson, Gary Fencik, Otis Wilson and Shaun Gayle all got regular media jobs in the Chicago market. Singletary—whose eyes defined intensity and were captured forever by NFL Films—Ron Rivera, Leslie Frazier, Ken Margerum and Richard Dent got into coaching.

Curiously, the player who pushed "The Super Bowl Shuffle," Willie Gault, moved away from the glare in search of bigger things in Hollywood. Little did he know the spotlight would remain in Chicago.

**HANDY DAN:** Dan Hampton tips a pass by Dallas' Danny White that deflected to Richard Dent, who ran it in for the Bears' first touchdown in their 44-0 rout.

**COMRADES IN ARMS:** In what would be the start of something big, Jim McMahon and Walter Payton walk to the locker room after a season-opening win over Tampa Bay.

**WHAT, THEM WORRY?** Walter Payton and Calvin Thomas joke with reporters at Super Bowl media day, Jim McMahon conducts a media session and Dennis Gentry, Stefan Humphries and Thomas try their hands as musicians in a taping of "The Super Bowl Shuffle."

"I don't think any of us realized the magnitude and staying power of just one season," said Gayle, a second-year player in 1985 who organized the '85 World Champions.

### 5. THE CONTROVERSY

When Ditka and Ryan had to be separated at halftime of the Miami loss, nearly coming to blows over whether linebacker Wilber Marshall should be covering receiver Nat Moore, the bizarre incident turned out to be just one round in a whole season of squabbles.

It began when defensive starters Al Harris and Todd Bell refused to sign new contracts and sat out all season. Ryan distrusted rookies, so to get Perry on the field more often, Ditka concocted the idea of using him at fullback. The Monday night debut against the Packers introduced a zaniness rarely experienced in pro sports.

Before that, McMahon and Ditka had been feuding over an injury, and McMahon implored Ditka to put him in against Minnesota on a Thursday night telecast. First pass, touchdown. Second pass, touchdown. Seventh pass, touchdown. Stuff like that just doesn't happen.

McMahon and Hampton got into it over the subject of playing through injury. McMichael, Hampton, Perry and Perry's wife got into it over who would appear in a tire ad.

When the Bears landed in New Orleans for the Super Bowl, McMahon stunned listeners by criticizing team President Mike McCaskey for refusing to allow Gault's acupuncturist on the team plane. McMahon later mooned a helicopter circling practice and was falsely accused of insulting New Orleans women.

Ditka made the mistake of allowing Perry instead of Payton to score in the Super Bowl and has paid for it ever since. Not often does a coach enjoy the luxury of designating touchdowns.

Is there anything else? No doubt. It's part of the deal. Two decades later, not every story has been told, every feud and all the funny business revealed. They have left the audience wanting more and remain poised to provide it.

### 6. UNIQUENESS

The Bears were a one-year dynasty. Lamenting that they never won again should not detract from the glory. The what-ifs should never drown out the what-was.

Besides, winning only once in such stunning, convincing fashion left an indelible mark on NFL history and crystallized the memory in ways the Bears of the '40s, the Browns and Lions of the '50s, the Packers of the '60s, the Steelers of the '70s, the 49ers of the '80s and the Cowboys of the '90s don't.

Those franchises are forced to sort out the seasons and the plays and the rosters and quarrel about which championship was best and exactly what happened in which year.

The Bears of 1986 went 14-2 and set a 16-game NFL record with 187 points allowed after Vince Tobin had replaced Ryan as coordinator. But it was never the same.

The 1985 Bears resonate with sports fans everywhere, firmly rooted and forever remembered among legendary American teams. It might be a weak rationalization, but it also just might be true that they couldn't have accomplished any more than they did.

JAM SESSION: Fans pack La Salle Street as team buses inch toward Daley Plaza for the Super Bowl victory rally.

# THE SEASON

# 15-1

An early rout of the Patriots. A memorable comeback at Minnesota. Payback in San Francisco. Back-to-back shutouts. A perfect NFC Central run. Only a loss to Miami stood between the Bears and a 16-0 regular season.

| | |
|---|---|
| **38-28**<br>SEPT. 8 VS. TAMPA BAY | **16-10**<br>NOV. 3 AT GREEN BAY |
| **20-7**<br>SEPT. 15 VS. NEW ENGLAND | **24-3**<br>NOV. 10 VS. DETROIT |
| **33-24**<br>SEPT. 19 AT MINNESOTA | **44-0**<br>NOV. 17 AT DALLAS |
| **45-10**<br>SEPT. 29 VS. WASHINGTON | **36-0**<br>NOV. 24 VS. ATLANTA |
| **27-19**<br>OCT. 6 AT TAMPA BAY | **24-38**<br>DEC. 2 AT MIAMI |
| **26-10**<br>OCT. 13 AT SAN FRANCISCO | **17-10**<br>DEC. 8 VS. INDIANAPOLIS |
| **23-7**<br>OCT. 21 VS. GREEN BAY | **19-6**<br>DEC. 14 AT NEW YORK JETS |
| **27-9**<br>OCT. 27 VS. MINNESOTA | **37-17**<br>DEC. 22 AT DETROIT |

**WHO'S NO. I?**
Bears coaches
Johnny Roland,
Ed Hughes and
Mike Ditka at work
during Win No. I
against Tampa Bay.

TWO-WAY PUNISHMENT: Jim McMahon strolls in for one of his two touchdowns, and safety Dave Duerson drops in on Buccaneers running back James Wilder during the Bears' opening victory.

# BALKY BEGINNING TURNS OUT WELL

## 21-point 2nd-half rally rescues season opener

A season of history began like anything but, with the underappreciated Bears offense bailing out the defense against what most considered a mediocre NFC Central opponent.

The Soldier Field crowd's expectations had been raised by a strong 10-6 season in 1984 followed by a playoff victory over Washington. But the Bears fell behind 28-17 at halftime as the Tampa Bay Buccaneers, not the Bears, were the smash-mouth team at the outset.

When it was over, Tampa Bay quarterback Steve DeBerg had thrown for three touchdowns to Jim McMahon's two, and Bucs running back James Wilder had outrushed Walter Payton 166 yards to 120. Wilder ran wild through a Buddy Ryan defense that was still feeling its way without Pro Bowl safety Todd Bell and defensive end Al Harris, both mired in contract impasses that would keep them out all season.

The Bucs scored first on a 1-yard pass to Calvin Magee, which the Bears answered with a 21-yard scoring pass from McMahon to Dennis McKinnon. But Kevin House scored from

SWEET SUHEY: Matt Suhey celebrates his third-quarter touchdown with Jay Hilgenberg and Dennis McKinnon.

44 yards out on another DeBerg pass. No one knew it then, but the Bucs would be the only team to score two first-quarter touchdowns against the Bears all season.

Jerry Bell gave the Bucs a 21-7 lead early in the second quarter on DeBerg's third scoring pass before a 1-yard McMahon run and a 38-yard Kevin Butler field goal brought the Bears within 21-17. However, Wilder powered into the end zone from 3 yards out for a 28-17 Tampa Bay lead at halftime. The defense then came to life and struck with what head coach Mike Ditka and others considered perhaps the most important play of the season.

Twenty-two seconds into the second half, cornerback Leslie Frazier read DeBerg's quick three-step drop and broke before the sideline pass was thrown. At the same time, defensive end Richard Dent detected signs of the play and drifted to his outside, into the path of the throw.

Dent deflected the pass, Frazier intercepted and the result was a 29-yard interception return for a touchdown that ignited the Bears. The TD brought them back within 28-24 and shifted all the momentum to them.

They took the lead for good when Matt Suhey made a diving catch of a McMahon pass for a 9-yard score and sealed it when Shaun Gayle blocked a punt to set up a 1-yard McMahon plunge for the final touchdown.

## 38 BEARS | 28 BUCCANEERS

### SEPT. 8, 1985, AT SOLDIER FIELD

**KEY PLAY:** Leslie Frazier's 29-yard interception return for a touchdown at the start of the third quarter. It trimmed Tampa Bay's lead to 28-24 and sparked the comeback.

**KEY STAT:** Bears gained 436 total yards, their second-best showing all season.

LOCKED UP:
Backup defensive
end Tyrone Keys
helps make life
miserable for
New England
quarterback
Tony Eason.

**THE RIGHT MAN:** Tight end Tim Wrightman racks up yards after catching one of his two passes against the Patriots.

# THINK THIS IS ONE-SIDED?

## A few months later, it would be worse

t would be a preview of Super Bowl XX. The Bears' defense utterly dominated the Patriots' offense, holding New England to 27 rushing yards. The Patriots keyed to stop Walter Payton and eventually sent him out of the game with bruised ribs, but myriad other Bears did sufficient damage.

The Bears sacked Tony Eason six times—they would sack Eason and Steve Grogan seven times in the Super Bowl—and held the New England offense to 206 yards, 90 coming on a late touchdown pass from Eason to Craig James. They forced the Patriots to punt 11 times, the same number of rushes New England would try in the Super Bowl.

The Bears opened the game with a decisive 69-yard drive that needed only four plays before Jim McMahon hit Dennis McKinnon with a 32-yard touchdown pass. Kevin Butler made the halftime lead 10-0 with a 21-yard field goal on a day when the offense hammered the Patriots with 44 runs to only 23 passes after a 34-34 run/pass balance the week before. The defense was swarming, with Mike Singletary blitzing and picking up three sacks to go with an interception.

Matt Suhey scored on a 1-yard dive in the third quarter, followed by a Butler field goal from 28 yards. The shutout was lost on the Eason-to-James touchdown, but the Bears otherwise completely outplayed their guests.

In a precursor to a bit of '85 Bears history, McMahon was replaced by Steve Fuller late in the game. McMahon's back was acting up; it required traction in the days before and after the game.

That would set the stage for the next Thursday in Minnesota, where McMahon was unable to start but came in to relieve Fuller with one of the legendary comeback performances of all time.

The Bears scored only one touchdown on four trips inside the New England 20. But for now they had to content themselves with what Buddy Ryan for much of the season would con-

| 20 | 7 |
|---|---|
| **BEARS** | **PATRIOTS** |

SEPT. 15, 1985, AT SOLDIER FIELD

**KEY PLAY:** Dennis McKinnon's 32-yard reception from Jim McMahon 3:03 into the game. The TD gave the Bears a 7-0 lead in a game in which they were never threatened.

**KEY STAT:** Bears held Patriots to 27 yards rushing.

sider the defense's best game. New England had rushed for 206 yards in its season opener; it totaled 206 yards in this game. The Bears completed 13 of 23 passes for 209 yards to go with the 160 on the ground in another demonstration that while attention rightly was being paid to the defense, there was more to the offense than just Payton left and Payton right.

**DOWN TIME:** Otis Wilson, Dave Duerson and Steve McMichael revel in a wicked hit on New England quarterback Tony Eason, who was sacked six times and threw three interceptions.

# McMAHON'S McMIRACLE

## His effort off bench is one to remember

This was the game that most point to as the difference-maker, the game that may have saved a season and certainly made the legend of Jim McMahon.

The Bears went into Minnesota with both division rivals sitting at 2-0. And for the second time in three games, the Bears would need a rescue.

It did not figure to come from McMahon. The quarterback had spent two nights in traction for his back problems and was suffering from a leg infection. He didn't practice in the short week leading up to the Thursday night game, and, despite McMahon's insistence that he would play, Mike Ditka had rules to the contrary.

McMahon had been injured late in the 1984 season and hadn't played in the Bears' playoff games against Washington or San Francisco. So in games of this magnitude, he remained an unknown commodity.

All that changed midway through the third quarter. With 7:32 to play and the Bears trailing 17-9, McMahon was in Ditka's ear along the sideline and finally persuaded the coach to send him in to replace Steve Fuller, who had simply been unable to spark a team that was being outplayed on both sides of the ball.

The Bears had taken leads in the first and second quarters with Kevin Butler field goals, but Minnesota went ahead 10-6 at halftime on a 14-yard pass from Tommy Kramer to Anthony Carter. Butler kicked a third field goal, but another Kramer TD pass boosted Minnesota to a 17-9 lead.

## 33 BEARS | 24 VIKINGS

SEPT. 19, 1985, AT THE METRODOME

**KEY PLAYS:** Jim McMahon's three touchdown passes in a span of 6:40 in the third quarter.

**KEY STATS:** Most productive games in careers of Willie Gault, who caught six passes for 146 yards, and Dennis McKinnon, who caught four for 133.

Enter McMahon. First play: McMahon pass to Willie Gault, 70 yards, touchdown. Second play: McMahon pass to Dennis McKinnon, 25 yards, touchdown. Before he was done, McMahon had completed 8 of 15 passes for a staggering 236 yards, including 43 on another touchdown pass to McKinnon, who accounted for 133 receiving yards.

Still, the Vikings got up off the canvas with a 57-yard touchdown pass from Kramer to Carter, bringing them within reach at 30-24. But Butler finished the scoring with a 31-yard field goal.

Overshadowed by McMahon's pyrotechnics were 127 rushing yards for the Bears and five turnovers forced by the defense. But the Bears had shown the nation emphatically that they were capable of being a quick-strike team as well as the NFL's dominant rushing offense behind Walter Payton.

---

**UP AND GOOD:** Jim McMahon can exhale after Kevin Butler's fourth field goal gives the Bears their final margin.

**FLYING LEAP:** Walter Payton, who gained only 6 yards rushing, bangs off a pair of defenders.

# ELECTRIC GAULT LIGHTS A CHARGE

## 31-point 2nd quarter turns deficit into win

**45** BEARS | **10** REDSKINS

SEPT. 29, 1985, AT SOLDIER FIELD

**KEY PLAY:** Willie Gault's 99-yard kickoff return for a touchdown. The play kick-started the Bears on a 31-point second-quarter outburst.

**KEY STAT:** Bears scored on five consecutive possessions in second quarter.

For most of the first quarter against Washington, the Bears looked like anything but the high-powered bunch that had blindsided the Vikings in the last game. They were outgained 141-2, and Walter Payton was on the way to a day that would give him 6 total yards on seven carries, one of the worst days of his career. They finished the afternoon with their fewest rushing yards, passing yards and first downs of the season, and they heard a smattering of boos. Jim McMahon was 0-for-4 and threw an interception in the first quarter.

But they finished the day 4-0 after handing the Redskins their worst beating in nearly 25 years.

What happened was another turning-point play, again involving Willie Gault, as it had

on the first McMahon miracle touchdown in Minnesota. With the Bears trailing 10-0 after a Mark Moseley field goal early in the second quarter, Gault took a Washington kickoff at his own 1-yard line and turned loose some of the legendary speed that made him a unique weapon for a unique team.

His touchdown sparked a 31-point blitz in the quarter as the defense completely shut down Joe Theismann's offense. After the Gault touchdown, the Redskins managed a total of 1 yard in their next three possessions, leaving the Bears with field position that set them up to score on drives of 14, 22 and 36 yards. McMahon passed to Dennis McKinnon 14 yards for a touchdown, followed that with a 10-yard TD pass to Emery Moorehead, then caught one of his own on a 13-yard heave from Payton.

What the game represented was the third time in four weeks that the Bears had rallied to win after trailing by more than seven points, and the result gave the Bears the NFL lead in

scoring. The Redskins outgained them 376-250, but the Bears were beginning to dominate offensively as much with McMahon's passing as with Payton's running.

McMahon threw a third touchdown pass in the third quarter, finding Payton for a 33-yard score, and Dennis Gentry ended the scoring with a 1-yard dive.

Washington had been a critical game in the 1984 playoffs, in which the Bears discovered and began to believe that they belonged on the same field with some of the NFL's best. Now they had gone a step further and confirmed that they were one of the NFL's best in their own right.

**ROLE REVERSAL:**
Jim McMahon grabs a touchdown pass from Walter Payton in the second quarter. McMahon had more luck than Redskins running back John Riggins, who is collared by Wilber Marshall.

**SQUEEZE PLAY:**
Mike Richardson and
Gary Fencik nail
Art Monk, who
coughs up the ball.

**CANNON CAN'T: Jim McMahon eludes Bucs defensive end John Cannon on a day when the quarterback rushed for 46 yards.**

# PICKED UP BY A PICKOFF

## Duerson's big play ignites turnaround

Once again the Bears struggled to get on track in a game they expected to win easily. In a near-replay of the season opener against Tampa Bay, the Bears trailed 12-3 at halftime and would have been shut out at intermission but for a 30-yard field goal by Kevin Butler as time expired in the second quarter.

It was not what the Bears had anticipated, certainly not against the winless Bucs. But there they were, looking up at the perennial doormats of the division. But just as they had in Game 1, the Bears used an interception to turn the momentum.

The first time it had been Leslie Frazier's pick. This time it was Dave Duerson breaking quickly on a ball intended for tight end Jimmy Giles, intercepting it and setting up a touchdown pass from Jim McMahon to Dennis McKinnon

covering 21 yards and pulling the Bears within 12-10.

The Bears then turned up the defensive pressure, and Tampa Bay quarterback Steve DeBerg pulled out from behind center too soon, leaving the ball on the ground. Defensive tackle Steve McMichael fell on it to set up another 30-yard Butler field goal to give the Bears their first lead.

They built the margin to 20-12 when Walter Payton, held under 100 yards rushing for the fourth straight game, scored on a 4-yard run in the fourth quarter.

Tampa Bay answered with a 25-yard touchdown pass by DeBerg, his second of the game, and suddenly it was 20-19 with five minutes to go.

McMahon twice talked coach Mike Ditka out of calling safe plays when it appeared that the easy way would be to punt and turn the game over to the defense. Instead McMahon converted a third-and-3 at the Bears' 24 with an 8-yard completion to Emery Moorehead to keep the ball and the drive alive.

With two minutes left, McMahon anticipated a Bucs blitz and went deep to Willie Gault for 48 yards to the Tampa Bay 11. Payton

## 27 | 19
**BEARS** | **BUCCANEERS**

OCT. 6, 1985, AT TAMPA STADIUM

**KEY PLAY:** Emery Moorehead's 8-yard reception on third-and-3 with the Bears up by one late in the fourth quarter. It led to Walter Payton's victory-clinching touchdown.

**KEY STAT:** Moorehead's eight receptions for 114 yards represented best day by a Bears tight end since Mike Ditka.

scored two plays later to clinch the game with his second touchdown, this from 9 yards.

The Bears were gaining confidence in their ability to rally using a variety of weapons, and Ditka was learning to let McMahon be McMahon. They were believing in their abilities, believing in their talent and, above all, believing in each other.

**FACE PLANT:**
Tampa Bay receiver
Gerald Carter pays
the price for
a reception as
Mike Singletary
gets a closer look.

CLOSE TO THE VEST: Willie Gault tries to control one of his three catches against the 49ers.

# PAYBACK PAYOFF: MEMORY ERASED

## Payton, Butler star; Montana takes a licking

| 26 | 10 |
|---|---|
| BEARS | 49ERS |

OCT. 13, 1985, AT CANDLESTICK PARK

**KEY PLAY:** In an affront to 49ers coach Bill Walsh, William Perry debuted at fullback on the final two plays of the game.

**KEY STAT:** Bears held offensive guru Walsh's attack without a touchdown for just second time in his career.

It was time for some payback against the last team that had beaten the Bears, and this time the Bears were ready, unlike the last time they'd visited the Bay Area.

The Bears had been shut out and humiliated 23-0 by the 49ers in the 1984 NFC championship game, which left the Bears aware of how much higher they needed to go to gain elite status but also aware that it was within their reach.

The Bears simply crushed the 49ers, even if the score was still 19-10 with just under four minutes to play. They sacked Joe Montana seven times, the most of his career to that point, and San Francisco managed only 45 total yards and three first downs in the second half.

But the story for the Bears was on offense, where Walter Payton and the line clicked into a new gear. Payton rushed for 132 yards, his season high so far, and carried the ball 24 times in the kind of performance that had been missing.

Significantly, the Bears opened the game passing, despite being without Dennis McKinnon and Emery Moorehead because of injuries. Jim McMahon accounted for 115 passing yards in the first quarter, and the offense scored the first four times it had the ball. Payton scored on a 3-yard run, and Kevin Butler converted three straight field goals as the Bears breezed to a 16-0 lead.

But the 49ers were Super Bowl champs, and Carlton Williamson returned an interception 43 yards for San Francisco's first score before Ray Wersching kicked a field goal from 32 yards.

But that was all the 49ers could manage against a team determined to get some payback for the 1984 thrashing. The Bears put away the game on a 29-yard Butler field goal in the fourth quarter and Payton's 17-yard touchdown run.

Coach Mike Ditka got a bit of payback of his own against San Francisco coach Bill Walsh, who had inserted guard Guy McIntyre as a fullback in the closing minutes of the title game. Ditka sent in defensive tackle William Perry as a running back and had him carry the ball on the final two plays, picking up 2 yards on each rush. The game ended, but Perry's time in the spotlight was only beginning.

# REFRIGERATOR IN THE LIVING ROOM

## Perry phenomenon too much for Packers

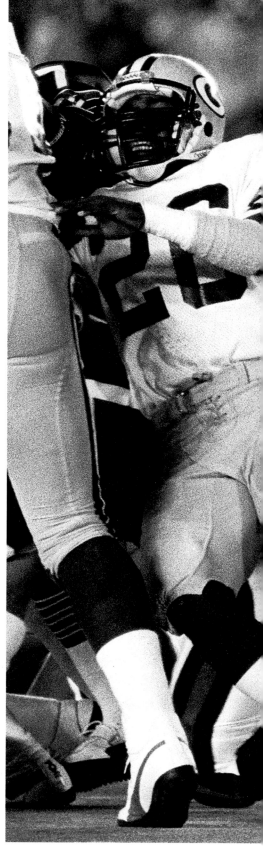

**W**hat had begun as an in-your-face gesture from Mike Ditka to Bill Walsh in Game 6 reached international proportions eight days later when William Perry, in front of a "Monday Night Football" audience, obliterated a Green Bay linebacker while blocking on two Walter Payton touchdowns and scored one of his own.

The Bears again trailed initially as Green Bay scored on a 27-yard pass from Lynn Dickey to James Lofton. But in the second quarter, the Bears exploded on the Packers, scoring 21 of the more memorable points in an absolutely memorable year.

With a first-and-goal situation at the Green Bay 2-yard line, Perry ran onto the field and lined up behind right tackle Keith Van Horne, with Payton behind Jim McMahon in the backfield. Perry then led Payton into the hole and met Green Bay linebacker George Cumby, who was at a 100-pound disadvantage. Perry bent Cumby backward, and Payton scored easily.

Several minutes later the Bears drove to the Green Bay 1-yard line, and Ditka again sent in Perry. But this time Perry was not blocking for Payton. Instead McMahon handed the ball to Perry, who rumbled into the end zone and then spiked the ball.

**PACK RAT: Randy Scott, who led the '85 Packers in tackles, separates Emery Moorehead from a second-quarter pass.**

| 23 | 7 |
|----|---|
| **BEARS** | **PACKERS** |

OCT. 21, 1985, AT SOLDIER FIELD

**KEY PLAY:** William Perry's 1-yard plunge in the second quarter, breaking a 7-7 tie. He also twice opened gargantuan holes for Walter Payton to score.

**KEY STAT:** Bears intercepted Green Bay quarterbacks Lynn Dickey and Randy Wright four times and knocked both out of game.

He was not finished. The Bears pushed the Packers backward one more time in the second quarter and again stood at the Green Bay 1. Ditka motioned to Perry, and the big rookie lumbered onto the field for a third time. Perry lined up behind the left guard and tackle and again found Cumby in the way, but not for long. Another crunching hit and Payton eased in for his second touchdown and one of his 112 rushing yards.

That was the end of the scoring by either offense, though Otis Wilson added the game's final points with a sack of backup quarterback Jim Zorn in the fourth quarter. The Bears fumbled seven times, losing four, but still outgained Green Bay 342-319. They held the Packers to 96 rushing yards while pounding the Packers for 175 of their own. McMahon completed only 12 of 26 passes for 144 yards, but the Bears intercepted four Green Bay passes to take away any offensive consistency from their guests.

But the night had belonged to Perry.

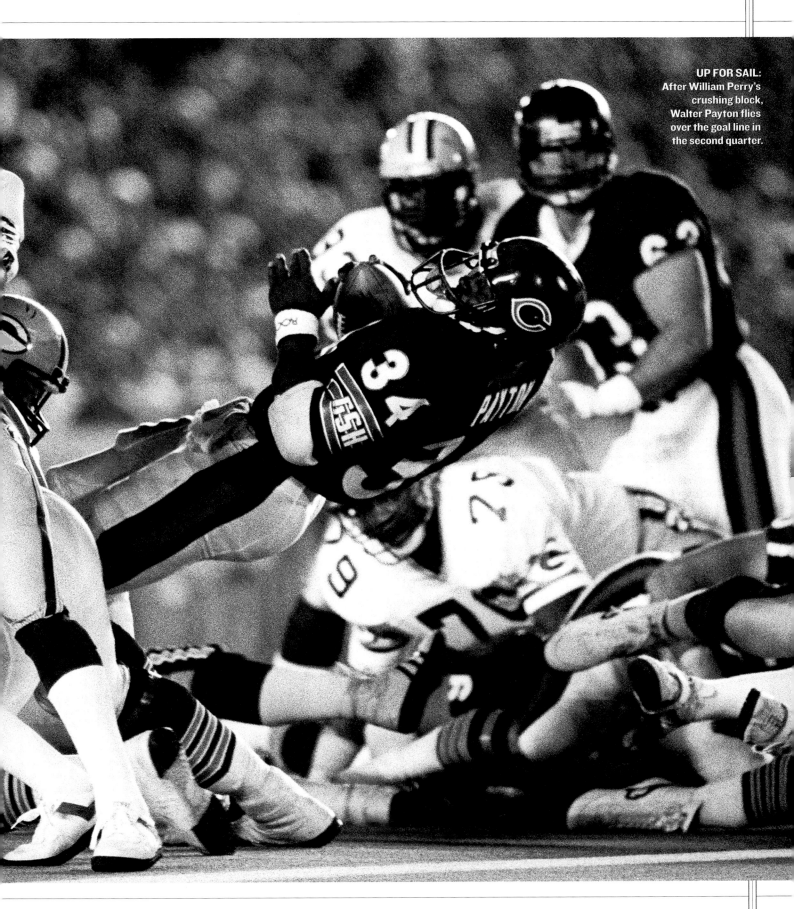

**UP FOR SAIL:**
After William Perry's crushing block, Walter Payton flies over the goal line in the second quarter.

# EVERY PHASE EARNS PRAISE

## 5 picked-off passes knock Vikes for loop

The Bears did not put themselves in another hole against Minnesota and need to turn to Jim McMahon, as they had in Game 3. This time they put away the Vikings early and kept them down in what some thought was one of their best games of the season.

McMahon struck with a 33-yard touchdown pass to Dennis McKinnon in the first quarter, and Kevin Butler made it 10-0 with a 40-yard field goal. Minnesota fought back with a 1-yard touchdown run by Darrin Nelson, but another Butler field goal put the Bears up 13-7 at halftime.

The Minnesota offense was done for the most part after that first score. The Bears' defense went on an interception frenzy against Tommy Kramer, the Minnesota quarterback who had been so effective against them in the first meeting, and backup Wade Wilson. The Bears' five interceptions gave them 21 through eight games, the same number they'd had for all of 1984. In fact, Otis Wilson returned one interception 23 yards for a touchdown in the third quarter.

The game marked the first real appearance of William Perry at defensive tackle. He recorded his first NFL sack and played well enough to be inserted into the starting lineup for the final eight games of the season. For all

**TEAM EFFORTS:** Mike Hartenstine helps Wilber Marshall to his feet after a Kevin Butler field goal, and Otis Wilson leads the cheers after a fourth-quarter sack of the Vikings' Tommy Kramer.

the attention paid to his time as a running or blocking back, this was the job he most wanted to do.

While the defense was holding the Vikings to 30 rushing yards, the Bears were getting Walter Payton 118 yards on 19 carries and 202 rushing yards as a team. This was Payton's third straight 100-yard game in what would be a record-setting stretch of 100-yarders.

The Bears amassed 413 yards of total offense, the fourth time in eight games they had topped 400 yards. At the midpoint of the season they were the NFL's only undefeated team and led in yards gained on offense and fewest allowed on defense.

The offense was continuing to stretch out in its distribution of the ball among backs, wide receivers and tight ends. Payton and Matt Suhey each caught five passes, Emery Moorehead four, Tim Wrightman two and McKinnon, Willie Gault and James Maness one apiece.

## 27 BEARS | 9 VIKINGS

### OCT. 27, 1985, AT SOLDIER FIELD

**KEY PLAY:** Otis Wilson's 23-yard interception return for a touchdown. It squelched a Minnesota rally and gave the Bears room to breathe at 20-7.

**KEY STAT:** Bears stuffed Vikings' running game, allowing only 30 yards.

# CIRCUS STARS: PERRY, PAYTON

## Packers bamboozled in contentious game

**S**ix personal fouls in the first half and a horde of cheap shots might have made it a pro wrestling match. William Perry's first touchdown catch might have made it a circus. Instead, Walter Payton turned the Bears' ninth straight victory into a personal tour de force. He matched the third-best performance of his career by rushing for 192 yards and sealed the Bears' closest victory of the season with a 27-yard touchdown run in the fourth quarter.

Payton's winning score came on an audible. Coach Mike Ditka had called for a pass to Payton to the left side, but when Jim McMahon saw the defense stacked, he changed the play to a run behind tackle Keith Van Horne on the right. Payton cut through the line, broke a tackle at the 20-yard line and outran the Green Bay secondary to the end zone. It was his 13th 100-yard performance in 20 games against the Packers, the 68th 100-yard game of his career and his fourth in a row.

| 16 | 10 |
|:---:|:---:|
| BEARS | PACKERS |

NOV. 3, 1985, AT LAMBEAU FIELD

**KEY PLAY:** Walter Payton's 27-yard touchdown run. It clinched the victory and kept the Bears undefeated.

**KEY STAT:** Payton ran for 192 yards on 28 carries.

**THAT'S A WRAP:** Walter Payton ends up in a bear hug from tackle Jim Covert after scoring on a 27-yard run, and Steve McMichael gets his arms around the legs of Green Bay quarterback Jim Zorn.

Payton's heroics were preceded by Perry's debut as a receiver. Trailing 3-0 early in the second quarter, the Bears sent Perry into the backfield. Payton had to tell him where to line up before the Refrigerator put his 308 pounds into slow motion toward the flat. Two weeks earlier, Perry had blasted Green Bay linebacker George Cumby into the end zone. This time Cumby was the victim again.

"They saw him coming and got out of the way," Ditka said.

Having been humiliated two weeks earlier in a Monday night loss featuring Perry's first TD run, the Packers decided to get down and, especially, dirty. Tempers flared repeatedly. Green Bay cornerback Mark Lee was ejected after he ran Payton out of bounds and completely over the bench. After another play had wound down, Packers safety Ken Stills leveled McMahon. Even so, Bears safety Dave Duerson acknowledged: "Let's face it. It wasn't clean on either side."

When the Bears arrived at their Lambeau Field locker room before the game, they found a bag of fertilizer from a Wisconsin radio station with the note: "Here's what you guys are full of." Payton aside, that might have been an appropriate odor for this game.

JERRY RICE? Hardly. But William Perry grabs a 4-yard touchdown pass during the Bears' victory at Lambeau Field.

**VIEWS TO A KILL:**
Matt Suhey, who rushed for 102 yards, rips off a large gain during the Bears' victory over the Lions as an injured Jim McMahon watches from the sideline.

# AGAINST FULLER, LIONS ON EMPTY

## Bears' offense clicks even without McMahon

J im McMahon sat this one out with tendinitis in his right shoulder, but Steve Fuller proved he could hand the ball off with the best of them as the Bears rolled to a 10-0 record. Walter Payton rushed for 107 yards and Matt Suhey for 102, the first time in two years that two Bears had broken 100 yards in the same game. The Bears ran 21 consecutive rushing plays before calling a pass, and they wound up running 55 times while throwing just 13. That made perfect sense. The Lions were the worst team in the NFL against the rush. Suhey proved that with six runs of 10 yards or more.

The William Perry extravaganza continued, though with a bit less flash. Late in the first quarter, the Bears had the ball at the 4-yard line. On came Perry. The Fridge lined up at left halfback and led the blocking, but Payton was stymied at the 2. The Bears needed seven plays, including a holding penalty against Detroit, to reach the end zone. Perry played on three of them, and he went in motion as a decoy on Fuller's 1-yard touchdown keeper.

Cold, misty Soldier Field weather gave both teams trouble holding on to the ball, as each side fumbled three times, losing two. Barely into the second quarter, the Lions already had fumbled twice and thrown an interception. Granted, the Lions did not present much

| **24** BEARS | **3** LIONS |
|---|---|

NOV. 10, 1985, AT SOLDIER FIELD

**KEY PLAY:** Steve Fuller's 1-yard TD run in the first quarter. Playing in place of the injured Jim McMahon, Fuller also scored the Bears' final touchdown.

**KEY STAT:** Bears outgained Lions by overwhelming 360-106 margin.

competition. But Buddy Ryan's defense held its fifth straight opponent to 10 or fewer points, forced four turnovers, recorded four sacks and gave up barely 100 total yards.

Still, Fuller deserves some credit. Not only did his offense outrush Detroit 250-68, he also outpassed Eric Hipple 112-73 and threw no interceptions to his opponent's two. Fuller also scored the first and last touchdowns on bootlegs. He did this without starting flanker Dennis McKinnon or starting tight end Emery Moorehead, who joined McMahon on the sidelines with injuries.

During warmups, McMahon tossed a few left-handed passes but did not test his right shoulder. It would be up to Fuller to lead the Bears for the next two games, in which they would post their most overwhelming victories … until the Super Bowl.

**TWIST-OFF CAP:**
Otis Wilson swivels the head of the Cowboys' Danny White during a third-quarter sack, knocking White from the game.

**LASSOED:** Even an assist from William Perry can't quite lift Walter Payton into the end zone.

# DITKA'S DELIGHT: DUMPING DALLAS

## Coach's roots make blowout win special

**M**ike Ditka played for Dallas for four years and coached there under Tom Landry for nine more. But perhaps no game had more meaning for him than the Bears' lopsided victory in Game 11. In Ditka's first regular-season visit to Texas Stadium since his coaching stint ended, his Bears handed the Cowboys their worst defeat in franchise history and their first shutout in 15 years.

How dominant was the Bears' defense? Midway through the fourth quarter of a 44-point uprising, the Bears had scored only one offensive touchdown. Richard Dent and Mike Richardson returned first-half interceptions for touchdowns, and punter Maury Buford continually pinned the Cowboys in uncomfortable positions.

The result: Dallas never penetrated beyond the Bears' 38-yard line. In fact, five of the Cowboys' first six running plays failed to achieve the line of scrimmage.

Early in the second quarter, linebacker Otis Wilson collared Danny White on a blitz. The quarterback was knocked out when he hit

the turf. White returned to start the second half, but Wilson knocked him out again. While White sat, the Bears tormented backup Gary Hogeboom into three interceptions.

Meanwhile, the offense put 378 total yards on the board and controlled the ball for 35:18, all with Jim McMahon sitting out again with a sore shoulder. Steve Fuller threw for 164 yards and kept a steady hand on the offensive throttle.

Late in the first half, Ditka sent William Perry into the offensive lineup. On first down from the 2, Perry took a handoff to the 1-yard line. Fuller plunged in on the next play, and it was 24-0 with nearly three minutes left until halftime. The rout was so complete that Ditka rested Fuller for the last 10 minutes in favor of rookie Mike Tomczak.

Kevin Butler kicked three field goals. His first was a career-long 44 yards. Then he bested that with a 46-yarder. Walter Payton gained 100 yards for the sixth game in a row, one short of the NFL record. He finished with 132 rushing yards on 22 carries.

The Bears' 11-0 start was the NFL's best since 1972 and allowed them to clinch the NFC Central with five weeks remaining. But Ditka's best memory had to be the sight of fair-weather Dallas fans streaming toward the exits after three quarters, their team hopelessly behind.

**OPEN ARMS:** Willie Gault catches a pass in front of Cowboys defender Ron Fellows.

| **44** | **0** |
|:---:|:---:|
| BEARS | COWBOYS |

NOV. 17, 1985, AT TEXAS STADIUM

**KEY PLAY:** Dan Hampton's force of a Danny White interception. The defensive end cartwheeled his blocker, jumped into White's face and batted the ball, which Richard Dent grabbed for the 1-yard touchdown that started the rout.

**KEY STAT:** Bears intercepted three passes in first half.

LINE DRIVE: Defensive lineman Mike Hartenstine grabs a fumble by Atlanta's Bob Holly.

# NUMBERS ADD UP TO AN EVEN DOZEN

## Payton, defense push Falcons into oblivion

After the Bears stomped Atlanta 36-0 at Soldier Field to complete a three-game stretch in which they'd outscored opponents by a combined 104-3, other numbers might pale. No way.

Walter Payton gained 102 yards for his seventh straight game with 100 or more yards, tying the NFL record held by Buffalo's O.J. Simpson and Houston's Earl Campbell. Payton, who left for the day in the third quarter, had his 71st career 100-yard game and scored the Bears' first touchdown by tiptoeing down the sidelines for 40 yards, the team's longest run of the season.

The defense suffocated the Falcons, holding them to 119 total yards and neutering the passing game. Atlanta's David Archer and Bob Holly combined to complete three passes for 16 yards, and their passing yardage was reduced to minus-22 when 38 yards of sacks were factored in.

Three of those sacks came from Henry Waechter, who recorded the Bears' third safety in six games.

Henry Waechter! Who knew?

The closest the Falcons penetrated was to the Bears' 18-yard line in the third quarter, but Gerald Riggs, the NFL's leading rusher, was held to 1 yard on a fourth-and-3 situation.

William Perry added a wrinkle to his offensive legend by scoring again, this time by leaping (everything's relative) into the end zone from the 1-yard line. Having been ankle-tackled and stopped short of the goal the previous week in Dallas, Perry took to the air this time after Steve Fuller had hit Willie Gault on consecutive passes of 20 and 50 yards. The touchdown was Perry's third of the season, second by rushing.

Normally sturdy fullback Matt Suhey hurt his back in the first half, and former Illini Calvin Thomas didn't miss a beat filling in. His 18-yard run helped set up the first of two Kevin Butler field goals, and Thomas himself scored on a 2-yard run in the second half.

The rout of the Falcons was the 12th consecutive victory for the Bears. Only two teams

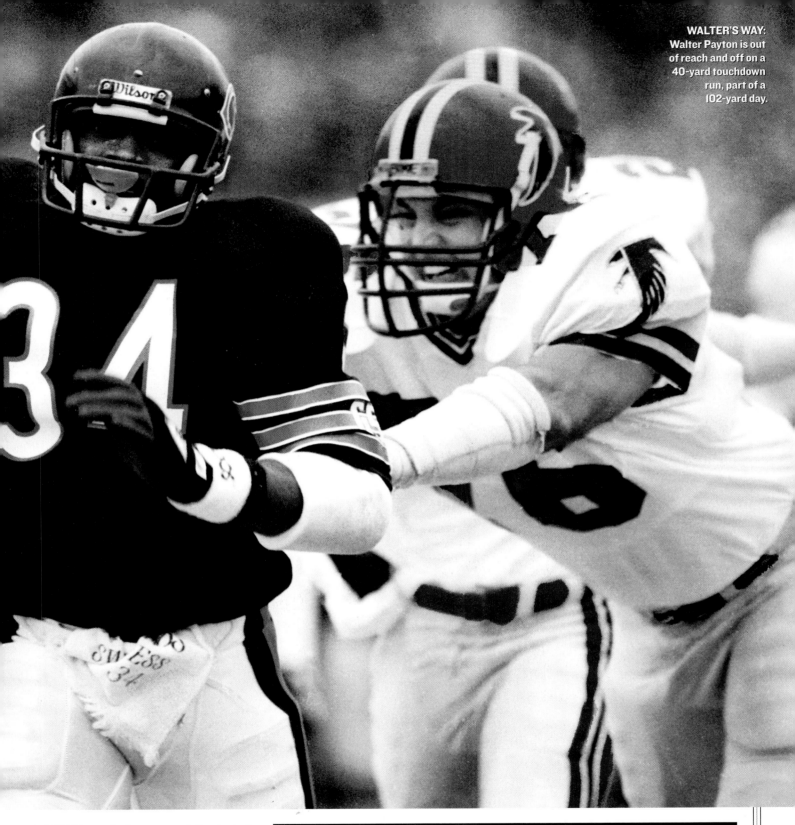

in NFL history had won more at the start of a season, the Bears' 13 in 1934 and the Miami Dolphins' 14 in 1972.

"Right now we're playing at a very high peak," defensive end Dan Hampton said. "We needed this type of effort to get ready for Miami because they're a great offensive team."

Eight days later, Hampton's words would prove prophetic.

## 36 | 0
**BEARS** | **FALCONS**

NOV. 24, 1985, AT SOLDIER FIELD

**KEY PLAYS:** Willie Gault's back-to-back 20- and 50-yard receptions from Steve Fuller. They brought the ball to the 1-yard line, and from there William Perry scored.

**KEY STATS:** Defense held Atlanta to minus-22 yards passing and had five sacks.

**GOING LIMP:**
Steve Fuller is helped
from the field after
spraining his ankle.

# ONE AND ONLY: SEASON SMUDGED

## Dolphins pile it on right from the start

Nobody's perfect, not even the 1985 Bears. When Miami had polished off the 38-24 victory that turned out to be the only blemish on the Bears' season, the Dolphins ensured that their 1972 record of 14-0 in the regular season and 17-0 overall would remain unequaled.

Seven seconds into the second quarter, the Bears trailed 17-7. Scoring on every first-half possession, Miami extended its lead to 31-10 at intermission. Mike Ditka chose to get into a shootout with the great Dan Marino in the first half, and Marino won. He wound up throwing for 270 yards and three touchdowns. Walter Payton, meanwhile, did not carry the ball until the Bears were behind 10-7 and nearly 10 minutes had elapsed.

One semi-highlight: Payton broke the NFL record with his eighth consecutive 100-yard game, but only because the Bears called time out three times on defense in the final minute after Payton had fumbled the ball away when he was stuck on 98 yards. But the Dolphins failed to run out the clock, and Payton got another chance, finishing with 121 yards.

"Walter Payton is the greatest football player to ever play the game," Ditka said. "Other people who call themselves running backs can't carry his jersey."

Jim McMahon had missed the previous three weeks with a tender shoulder, but he looked sharp in warmups. Still, Ditka left him on the bench until Steve Fuller sprained his ankle early in the fourth quarter. McMahon moved the Bears briefly until throwing an interception with 6:12 to go. It was Miami's third

**A SINGLE(TARY) LOSS:** Linebacker Mike Singletary and the defense had no answer for Dan Marino and the Dolphins in the Bears' only defeat.

interception against a team that had thrown just nine during its 12-0 start.

Not all the action was on the field. When the Bears gave up their fourth touchdown in the first half after a blocked punt at their own 6-yard line, Ditka screamed in frustration at Buddy Ryan on the sidelines. But Ditka was calm, even cocky, postgame: "Nobody's perfect, and we proved it. Now it's what you do with it. Do you bounce back? We'll be back. [The Dolphins] deserved to win and we didn't. I hope they go as far as we're going to go and we play them again."

Of course, the Dolphins did not go to the Super Bowl. But the next day several Bears did record "The Super Bowl Shuffle." Perfect season or not, this team had swagger.

## 24 BEARS | 38 DOLPHINS

DEC. 2, 1985, AT THE ORANGE BOWL

**KEY PLAY:** Maury Buford's punt being blocked at the Bears' 6-yard line. Nat Moore's ensuing touchdown made it 31-10 Miami, still in the first half.

**KEY STAT:** Dolphins' 31 first-half points were most against Bears since 1972 season opener.

**BEACHED:**
Leslie Frazier and Wilber Marshall join forces to stop Colts tight end Pat Beach.

# UGLY, BUT THEY'LL TAKE IT

## Sluggish Bears have enough to win eyesore

Turns out meaningless games were not meaningless to championship-starved Soldier Field fans, who showered a 12-1 team with boos at halftime of a listless effort against Indianapolis. The Bears already had clinched home-field advantage throughout the playoffs but no longer could go undefeated, so they lacked motivation for the final three games the schedule said they had to play. Still, a 17-10 victory was better than the reverse.

Predictably, the Bears came out flat. Problem was, they stayed that way until a couple of time-consuming drives in the second half stuck the Colts on the shelf.

Jim McMahon returned from sick bay and started for the first time in five weeks. He said his shoulder felt fine, but he was nothing special with an 11-of-23 afternoon for 145 yards and no touchdowns.

Walter Payton came through late in the third quarter to break a 3-3 halftime tie with a 16-yard touchdown run.

Steady as ever, he extended his NFL record by gaining 100 yards for the ninth game in a row. He ran 20 times in the second half after only six in the first half because, coach Mike Ditka said, he "got nasty notes from the media saying, 'Run Payton.'"

Fighting the effects of the flu, Payton finished with 111 yards, yet he said his most satisfying moment had been "a block for Matt Suhey."

Actually, on a day devoid of big plays for the Bears, Calvin Thomas wound up scoring the clinching touchdown on a 3-yard scamper with six minutes left.

That offset an ensuing 61-yard Mike Pagel-to-Wayne Capers pass on which cornerback Mike Richardson got undressed.

The defense forced concern by failing to force a turnover for the first time all season. That made Maury Buford the day's most valuable player, as he booted terrific punts to the 4-yard line to set up both touchdowns.

"Wasn't fancy, but it's 13-1," said linebacker Otis Wilson, who recorded the Bears' only sack late in the game.

In the Bears' last home appearance before the playoffs, even a sluggish effort was enough to propel them to their 13th victory, which tied the franchise record set in 1934.

"I'm not unhappy," Ditka said. "I didn't think it would be a blowout like a lot of people. The main thing is we're going into the playoffs, and people are going to have to come here to play us."

After enduring this stinker, fans would say the playoffs could come none too soon.

**LOW BRIDGE: Richard Dent hovers over Indianapolis quarterback Mike Pagel after leveling him in the fourth quarter.**

| 17 | 10 |
|:---:|:---:|
| **BEARS** | **COLTS** |

### DEC. 8, 1985, AT SOLDIER FIELD

**KEY PLAY:** Walter Payton's 16-yard touchdown run late in the third quarter. He rushed for more than 100 yards for the ninth straight game.

**KEY STAT:** For only time all season, Bears had no takeaways or giveaways.

# BUDDY SYSTEM: CLASS IN SESSION

## Ryan's students get it right again

Everyone knew that the Bears were dominating with their defense. But, ever the skeptic and bothered by mediocre performances the previous two games, coordinator Buddy Ryan turned classroom proctor. In the week leading up to the Jets game, Ryan gave his players three written tests on the game plan. It proved the value of cramming for finals. The Bears limited their 11th opponent to 10 or fewer points and allowed zero touchdowns for the fourth time as they hammered the Jets 19-6 in East Rutherford, N.J. Their stamp was clear when sizing up the Jets' third quarter. New York's five drives netted 0, 6, 2, 4 and 4 yards. "Our defense took the game away," Mike Ditka said.

Especially Richard Dent. The lanky defensive end punctuated that superior third quarter by climbing on the back of quarterback Ken O'Brien, at that time the NFL's leading passer, and knocking the ball out of his arm on sacks that ended consecutive possessions. Dent also abused New York left tackle Reggie McElroy so much that he was driven out of the game.

As the Bears won 14 games for the first time in franchise history, the offense was not outstanding. But in the cold, windy weather, it got the job done by controlling the ball for an incredible 39 minutes 36 seconds. Tight

**M & M'S:** Tight end Emery Moorehead looks for running room after a catch, and linebacker Jim Morrissey closes in to tackle a Jets receiver.

end Tim Wrightman's first career touchdown reception and four field goals by Kevin Butler provided more than enough for the stellar defense. Butler's second field goal was his 26th of the season, breaking the club record Mac Percival set in 1968. His last one broke Bob Thomas' team record of 11 in a row. That 21-yard chip shot came with just 17 seconds left in a contest that already had been decided, though Ditka denied he was rubbing it in. "We were just going for the record," he said.

However, Walter Payton no longer was going for a record. His streak of 100-yard rushing games ended at nine after the Jets held him to 53 yards on 28 carries. New York stopped him for a loss or no gain 11 times. "They were the best defense we've faced," center Jay Hilgenberg said. Payton did catch a 65-yard pass that set up the field goal on which Butler passed Percival.

So the Bears went into a hostile city, played in nasty weather, contained a potent offense … and weren't satisfied. "No question we've got to play better," Jim McMahon said. But how to stay motivated? Said defensive lineman Dan Hampton, "You don't need any motivation except pride."

## 19 BEARS  6 JETS

### DEC. 14, 1985, AT GIANTS STADIUM

**KEY PLAY:** Jim McMahon's 65-yard pass against the wind to Walter Payton in the pivotal third quarter. It set up a Kevin Butler field goal that gave the Bears a 13-6 edge.

**KEY STAT:** Butler accounted for all but six points with field goals of 18, 31, 36 and 21 yards, plus an extra point.

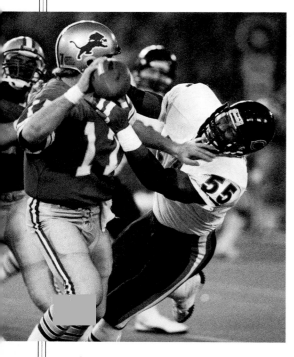

**UNWANTED GUESTS:** Otis Wilson is an unpleasant backfield visitor, sacking Detroit's Eric Hipple. And Dennis Gentry tightropes the sideline and holds the ball aloft at the end of his 94-yard kickoff return.

# MANY STARS OF THIS SHOW

## Lots of contributors help end on right note

On paper, a 20-point victory over a division rival to end the regular season 15-1 would seem to provide a springboard into the playoffs. But these were the '85 Bears, who could find something wrong with a $100 bill. For instance: It took the Bears more than 46 minutes to score an offensive touchdown. They turned the ball over four times, three on interceptions and once on a fumble.

They managed just two touchdowns on eight trips inside the Detroit 30-yard line. They failed by four points to break the 1978 Pittsburgh Steelers' record for points allowed in a 16-game schedule, finishing with 198.

They watched inspirational leader Mike Singletary limp off the field with a sprained left knee.

Even though coach Mike Ditka berated his team after the victory at the Pontiac Silverdome, the Bears had become just the second squad in NFL history to win 15 games in the regular season and the first in a dozen years to go unbeaten in the NFC Central. They finished second in the league in points scored and first in total defense, first in rushing defense and third in passing defense.

Many individuals merited notice, even the grouchy Ditka, who matched Bill Walsh as the only coaches with 15 wins in a season. The incomparable Walter Payton became the first man with more than 2,000 yards in combined rushing and receiving yardage three years in a row.

The first of Kevin Butler's three field goals gave him 134 points for the season and broke

Gale Sayers' NFL rookie scoring record set 20 years earlier. Ron Rivera, replacing the injured Singletary, became the 21st Bear to score by returning a recovered fumble 5 yards in the fourth quarter.

Dennis Gentry electrified his team by returning the second-half kickoff 94 yards for a touchdown that busted open a tight 6-3 contest. Wilber Marshall creamed Joe Ferguson so hard on a rollout that the Lions quarterback's arms dangled at his side before he hit the ground.

Laughter was provided in the fourth quarter when William Perry, who had forced James

# 37
**BEARS**

# 17
**LIONS**

**DEC. 22, 1985, AT THE SILVERDOME**

**KEY PLAY:** Dennis Gentry's 94-yard kickoff return for a TD to open the second half. The play helped turn a 6-3 lead into a rout.

**KEY STAT:** Bears recovered four Detroit fumbles and picked off three interceptions.

Jones to cough up the ball earlier in the game, scooped up a fumble and trudged some 40 hilarious yards downfield before being hauled down inside the Detroit 20. That set up Jim

McMahon's 11-yard pass to Ken Margerum for the final touchdown of an irregular regular season.

Now the playoffs—and history—awaited.

**ROAD GRADER:** With Jay Hilgenberg leading the interference, Walter Payton picks up some of his 93 yards against the Giants.

# KNOCKED COLD

## Stout defense as nasty as weather in demolition of Giants

After shutting down the defending champion 49ers in the wild-card playoff game, the New York Giants believed they had a chance against the Bears in the NFC semifinals at Soldier Field. Fat chance.

Sean Landeta whiffed on a punt when a gust of wind blew the ball off his foot in the first quarter, and Shaun Gayle ran it in for a bizarre 5-yard touchdown. Then Jim McMahon threw two third-quarter touchdown passes to Dennis McKinnon, and the Bears won comfortably 21-0.

But the story of the game—the story of the season—was the Bears' defense, as cold-hearted as the weather that chilled 62,076 delighted spectators. The Giants went three-and-out on nine of their first 11 possessions. Running back Joe Morris managed just 32 yards on 12 carries, 14 of those yards on his first attempt. Phil Simms was sacked six times. Before piling up 129 yards on their final two garbage-time drives, the Giants averaged less than 2 yards per play, and they were 0-for-12 on third-down conversions.

Buddy Ryan had promised a shutout, and his players delivered.

"We believe every thought Buddy shares with us," safety Dave Duerson said.

Defensive tackle William Perry set the tone, nailing Morris behind the line with a brutal hit that forced the 5-foot-7-inch running back from the game for a time with a mild concussion. "I got him with everything I had," Perry said.

The Giants came into the game with the No. 2-ranked defense in the NFL but left knowing the chasm separating them from the Bears was substantial. "Our defense—you've got to love them," coach Mike Ditka said. "Buddy did a great job coaching them."

Richard Dent led that defense with six tackles and 3½ sacks, spending the entire afternoon in Simms' face.

"They didn't know who to block," linebacker Wilber Marshall said. "That's what makes this defense so exciting. It's so complicated nobody

**EYES ON THE PRIZE:**
Mike Singletary
closes in on
New York's
Phil Simms, who
was sacked six times.

**PUNT STUNT:** After Sean Landeta's phantom punt results in a 5-yard touchdown for Shaun Gayle (23) in the NFC semifinal, Bears players and fans go wild.

can figure it out." Gayle became the ninth Bears defender to score this season with "my first touchdown since high school."

Meanwhile, the offensive line did not allow a sack to a Giants pass rush that led the league in sacks, completely neutralizing All-Pro linebacker Lawrence Taylor, who spent most of the fourth quarter on the sideline screaming in frustration.

McKinnon, who had three catches for 52 yards, first roused Taylor's ire with a devastating but legal crackback block on a first-quarter running play. He later mixed it up with Giants cornerback Elvis Patterson, whom he beat for both his touchdown catches.

"They call him Toast because he gets burned so often, right?" McKinnon said. "I didn't have toast for breakfast, but I had it for dinner."

The Bears' offense had no penalties or turnovers. With Walter Payton running for 93 yards, the Bears amassed 363 yards, which was 93 more than the Giants had been allowing.

"It wasn't easy," Ditka said. "Nothing in life

# 21 | 0
**BEARS** | **GIANTS**

NFC SEMIFINAL
JAN. 5, 1986, AT SOLDIER FIELD

**KEY PLAY:** After Sean Landeta whiffed on a first-quarter punt, Shaun Gayle's 5-yard return gave the Bears a 7-0 lead that was more than enough.

**KEY STAT:** The Giants went three-and-out on nine of their first 11 possessions and were 0-for-12 on third-down conversions.

is easy, but our players were on a mission. We beat a good football team."

No, they completely manhandled a good football team. What does that say about the Bears?

# SUPER SMOOTH SAILING

## Defense, cold send Bears on way to New Orleans for 1st Super Bowl

**B**uddy Ryan had so much confidence in the Bears' impregnable, take-no-prisoners defense that he predicted three fumbles by Rams All-Pro running back Eric Dickerson in the NFC championship game. Ryan was wrong. Dickerson fumbled just twice. "If they would have run him more," Ryan scoffed, "he would have had three."

When Bear weather—frigid temperatures, howling winds and swirling snow flurries—descended on Soldier Field, the Bears knew their first Super Bowl ticket was pretty well punched. In those conditions, Dickerson was the Southern California visitors' only hope. And he couldn't deliver, managing just 46 yards on 17 carries.

Worse, by falling behind 10-0 in the first 10 minutes 34 seconds, the Rams were forced to play catch-up, and they had no chance against a defense that seemed to know what they were going to do before they even tried it and responded with ferocious effectiveness in a 24-0 thumping. Overwhelmed quarterback Dieter Brock completed just 10 of 31 passes for 66 yards with one interception. He was sacked three times and spent the entire afternoon running for his life.

When did the Bears seize control? "Kickoff," said Dan Hampton, centerpiece of the defensive line that thwarted Dickerson and intimidated Brock. Early on, Hampton could see defeat in the Rams' faces. "I can tell by looking in their eyes whether they want to play or not," he said. "I knew they weren't really sure they wanted to be in Chicago playing us."

The Bears, who became the first team in NFL history to record back-to-back shutouts in the playoffs, were just as efficient if not as spectacular on offense, most notably Jim McMahon.

The punky QB completed 16 of 25 throws for 164 yards, running for one touchdown when he was supposed to pass and passing for another touchdown when he was supposed to hand off. He threw against the wind and with the wind and through the wind in a performance that drew superlatives from hard-to-please coach Mike Ditka.

"You don't understand how well our quarterback threw the football," Ditka said. McMahon's favorite target was Walter Payton, who gained only 32 yards rushing but added 48 yards on seven receptions.

After the Rams went three-and-out on their first possession, McMahon took the Bears 56 yards in five plays for a 7-0 lead, scoring the touchdown on a 16-yard run. Kevin Butler added a 34-yard field goal before the first quarter ended, and the tone of the day was set.

McMahon converted Dickerson's second fumble into a 22-yard TD pass to Willie Gault in the third quarter, waving off the draw play Ditka had sent in from the sidelines.

The defense got into the offensive act in the fourth quarter, Wilber Marshall returning Brock's fumble 52 yards for the game's final

**GOT HIS BACK:** Offensive guard Mark Bortz blocks the Rams' Gary Jeter as Jim McMahon prepares to pass.

score after Brock had been dumped for the third time.

How one-sided was it? The Rams' longest drive was 27 yards. They went three-and-out on eight of their 16 possessions and averaged just 2.2 yards per play.

"I don't want to sound like I'm not happy about what happened today," Ditka said. "But we're on a mission, and it won't be finished until we're finished in New Orleans."

## 24 BEARS | 0 RAMS

NFC CHAMPIONSHIP
JAN. 12, 1986, AT SOLDIER FIELD

**KEY PLAY:** Willie Gault's 22-yard touchdown reception. Jim McMahon waved off Mike Ditka's call for a draw play and hit Gault, who had faked cornerback LeRoy Irvin inside and then run a corner route.

**KEY STATS:** The Rams' longest drive covered 27 yards. They averaged 2.2 yards per play.

**MEN OF THE HOUR:** Hallmarks of the Bears' run to the NFC championship were the rugged defense of linemen Steve McMichael (76) and Dan Hampton (99) and the insouciance of quarterback Jim McMahon, sporting his famous "Rozelle" headband.

# MERCY!

## 46 points, '46' defense add up to utter domination

The Bears were far and away the most dominant team in football in 1985, so it was only appropriate that they wrapped up a storybook season with the most dominant performance in Super Bowl history. After taking Bourbon Street by storm during a week of frenzied buildup, they turned their attention to football and pulverized the New England Patriots 46-10 at the New Orleans Superdome. The game was so one-sided it evoked comparisons with an earlier Bears team's 73-0 destruction of the Washington Redskins in the 1940 NFL title game, football's previous standard for utter annihilation.

"Right now I'm so happy I could jump up to the top of the Superdome," All-Pro linebacker Mike Singletary said after orchestrating a defensive effort that drove New England quarterback Tony Eason from the game after six feeble possessions.

The Patriots actually scored first, converting a fumble into a field goal after Jim McMahon and Walter Payton missed connections on a handoff. The short-lived 3-0 lead deprived the Bears of an opportunity for a third straight postseason shutout. But by the time backup QB Steve Grogan got the Pats on the board again, it was 44-3. Grogan was then sacked for a fourth-quarter safety, making the 46-10 final score especially poignant because it was the "46" defense the Bears used to lay waste to the NFL all season.

"The game was never in question," coach Mike Ditka said.

Ditka, the star tight end on the Bears' last championship team in 1963, joined the Raiders' Tom Flores as the only men to play for and coach a Super Bowl champion. Ditka said he'd cherish this ring more, while remaining in debt to franchise founder George S. Halas, the late Papa Bear, who coached the '63 champions and who gave Ditka the chance to coach the Bears.

"What you do in life by yourself doesn't mean as much as what you accomplish with a group of people," Ditka said. "It's because of Mr. Halas that I'm here. I'm just trying to pay some dues."

McMahon, whose antics in the week leading up to the game left him a marked man, responded with the sort of insouciant effectiveness that characterized his play all season. He completed 12 of 20 passes for 256 yards, setting up his own two touchdown runs and a third by Matt Suhey. "We could have got to 60 points, but we ran out of time," McMahon said. "And I would like to have seen a goose egg up there for them."

Willie Gault caught four passes for 129 yards, and charismatic 308-pound rookie William Perry bulldozed through the dazed Pats for his fourth touchdown of the season in the third quarter. That score, though, ignited the game's biggest controversy. Walter Payton, the proud face of the Bears franchise in some of its bleakest years, was denied an opportunity to score a Super Bowl touchdown. Payton led the Bears with 61 yards on 22 carries but failed to score.

"I wanted to get Walter into the end zone," Ditka insisted. "But our plays are designed to score, and I didn't know who had the ball."

"I feel very sad for No. 34," McMahon said.

Hurt feelings aside, it's a safe bet the Bears could have won without Payton and McMahon,

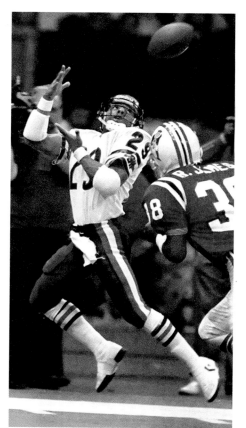

**CATCH AND RELEASE: Dennis Gentry hauls in a pass to the I-yard line to set up a third-quarter touchdown, and Otis Wilson, Wilber Marshall and Dan Hampton unstack from Tony Eason after a sack.**

so superior was their defense. They held the AFC champions to 123 total yards and 12 first downs, none in the first 25 minutes.

The defense also contributed to the point barrage when rookie cornerback Reggie Phillips returned a third-quarter interception 28 yards

**LEAVING A DENT:**
Super Bowl MVP
Richard Dent knocks
the ball loose from
Craig James in the
first quarter.

**CLOUD NINE:**
Jim McMahon
and the Bears were
the champions.

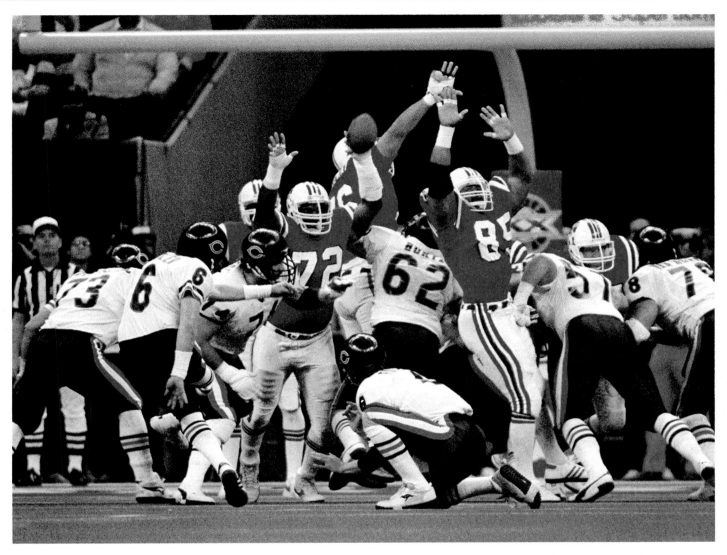

## 46 | 10

**BEARS** | **PATRIOTS**

JAN. 26, 1986, AT THE SUPERDOME

**KEY PLAY:** William Perry's third-quarter touchdown. Some of the Bears never forgave Mike Ditka for calling the Fridge's number instead of Walter Payton's from the 1-yard line.

**KEY STAT:** 46-10. Total domination.

for a touchdown. Defensive end Richard Dent, leader of the pass rush that sent Eason scurrying for cover, was voted the Super Bowl's Most Valuable Player, but the Bears would have been just as happy if the award had gone to Buddy Ryan, architect of their fearsome defense.

"Buddy is the MVP of our defense," Singletary said. "He's a step ahead of everybody else. If it wasn't for him, what happened today wouldn't have happened. He's a real genius."

Singletary and his cohorts showed their appreciation at the final gun. As Ditka was being carried off the field, several defensive players hoisted Ryan to their shoulders and accorded him a similar tribute.

"I can't tell you how I feel about these guys," Ryan said. "They started off terrible this year. They gave up 28 points in the first game and were ranked 25th in the league. But they kept working like dogs to get it done. They did everything they could to be No. 1. That's what makes me so proud of these kids.

"This is the best defense that I've ever been with, and I've been with some awful good ones."

**SCORING ... OR NOT:** Under New England pressure, Kevin Butler knocks through one of his five Super Bowl extra points. Not so fortunate was Walter Payton, who rushed for 61 yards but did not get a touchdown.

**BULK DELIVERY:**
William Perry
dives for a I-yard
touchdown that
added controversy to
Super Bowl XX.

**END-ZONE ENDING:**
Cornerback
Reggie Phillips
charges in with a
28-yard interception
for a touchdown.

**CHAT ROOMS: Dennis Gentry and Calvin Thomas (top) shout in celebration while Bears President Michael McCaskey talks with Walter Payton near Jim McMahon and Kevin Butler.**

**SACK TIME:**
Dan Hampton
and Otis Wilson
celebrate some
rough treatment
of Steve Grogan.

**SHOUTING TILL THEY'RE HOARSE:** Chicago police use equine assistance to keep control of raucous
Bears fans during celebrations on the North Side that included overturning a car.

**FLAGGED FOR CELEBRATION:** An embellished Chicago city flag is carried through the streets.

**PARADE ROOT:** Bears fans cheer their heroes on the slow procession to Daley Plaza.

**STANDING ROOM ONLY:** Players and fans ride atop the team buses as the ticker-tape parade makes its way through an estimated 500,000 fans to a rally in Daley Plaza the day after the Bears won the Super Bowl.

**RAISES FOR ALL!** Bears President Michael McCaskey shows off the Super Bowl trophy while Tom Thayer cheers during the rally.

**BOOZE BROTHERS:** An oversize champagne glass seems a great way for a fan to toast the championship.

*Interviews by* STEVE ROSENBLOOM
*Portraits by* CHARLES CHERNEY

# Mike Ditka

THEN: Head coach  NOW: Restaurateur

**46-10.** That's what I remember. The scoreboard.

**The feeling** I had was relief that it was over because it takes so much out of you leading up to that game.

**I had** such a magnificent group of guys. They're the neatest guys.

**They captured** the imagination of everybody. One reason was, I never reined them in. I let them go. I let their personalities show. I let their character show. You are what you are as people. We all have emotions. Show them. Have fun.

**The greatest,** on and off the field.[1] The best-conditioned athlete I've ever been around. The biggest practical joker I've ever been around. A leader by example. The one guy on our team that everybody on our team admired.

**He hadn't** practiced all week.[2] I didn't think he could throw the ball. He started driving me crazy, wanting to play.

**So we** get behind, he's still going nuts, and after the half I put him in. And I knew what was going to happen. I assumed that they thought he couldn't throw the ball, because that's what I thought. So the first play, he read the defense, he knew it was a blitz, he had man-to-man outside, he audibles to the fly route, Willie[3] gets it, and bang.

**He isn't** in the game five seconds, and touchdown. How dumb do I look?

**He throws** three in a period of about five minutes.

**We had** a lot of fun with him.[4] And the players loved it because "Is he going to run this week? Is he going to catch? Is he going to pass?" We had a little bit of everything. We made a circus out of it. We made the kid famous.

**He[5] was** going to attack you. He was going to make you break down somewhere if you couldn't protect it. When you do it, you're man-to-man all the time. I used to look at film and see guys that would be open everywhere, but the quarterback was laying on the ground.

**My dad** was really strict. I was the oldest child, and my dad took most of the frustration out on me. He was in the Marines.

**I was** always the kid who got in trouble. For some reason, it just found me. Little things. So I got whipped a lot.

**My mom** is great to this day. I was her favorite because I was the firstborn. I always tell my brothers and sister that, anyway.

**I was** a much better baseball player.

**They came** back to me and asked me if I'd get involved, and I said I would.[6] They asked, "Do you want a position?" I said, "No, I don't want a position. I don't want to walk around and tell anybody what to do. Let me observe for a while, and then if I have a suggestion, I'll give it to you."

**This is** what football was when I started playing. We didn't make any money. We went out and played. These guys play offense, defense, special teams.

**I have** Super Bowl rings from Dallas. I have league championship rings. I have Hall of Fame rings. This[7] means something to me because I had a vision and I watched it come true. What Jim Finks put in place, what Jerry[8] and I put in place, and Bill Tobin, it was phenomenal.

**The best** thing I ever did was draft Jim Covert at left tackle. I think he's one of the best I've ever seen.

**At the** end of my career, the wizard[9] came in and made a lot of the calls, and did just terrible drafting.

**I think** I found out that as many people don't like you as like you. I don't think there's a more genuine person in the world than me. Now, whether people understand that or not, I don't care.

**What did** I do wrong? They won two championships in this town in 50 years, and I played on one and coached the other one. I'll go somewhere and apologize, but you'll have to tell me where and who to.

**In the** locker room in 1984 after we got [beat] by the 49ers, I told those guys, "You come back next year and you take care of the 49ers, and I'll take care of the 49ers' coach."

1. Walter Payton.
2. Jim McMahon before the Thursday night game against Minnesota.
3. Willie Gault.
4. William "The Refrigerator" Perry.
5. Buddy Ryan.
6. Buying into the Rush of the Arena Football League.
7. His Bears Super Bowl ring.
8. Former general manager Jerry Vainisi.
9. Michael McCaskey.

# Dan Hampton

THEN: No. 99, defensive end  NOW: Hall of Famer

**Our Super** Bowl was played against the Giants and then the Rams, because we knew once we got to the Super Bowl, it was an avalanche. No one was going to stop us.

**It was** an amazing anticipation of all the expectations. Boom. It's done. It's over. We've done it.

**A lot** of times people become overwhelmed and intimidated by something that explodes, and the next thing you know, it's on national TV. It was like Ditka took it in stride, saying, "OK, that's great." It's almost a Machiavellian way of using the Fridge on the "Monday Night Football" game. It's almost like he orchestrated it.

**Buddy fostered** an us-against-the-world mentality.

**The moment** of truth was the Miami game, and you know about them grabbing each other in the shower and starting fisticuffs.

**Actually, Ditka** was right. Ditka was right in saying, "Hey, whatever you thought, it ain't working. You've got to change."

**Twenty years** later, that still is the gold standard. When I played, everybody talked about the "Steel Curtain" and the "Doomsday Defense." Now, 20 years later, they talk about the Bears' defense.

**You're not** going to run it on us. When you try to throw it on us, it's just a matter of time before we start tearing your quarterback down.

**You have** to give a lot of credit to Jim Finks in that he was able to build a roster of talent that Ditka was able to utilize.

**I had** five operations on each leg when I played, and when I finished, I had both of them done again, so that's 12. I'll need some type of artificial joint when I'm 55 or 60.

**I couldn't** run out of the house if it was on fire, but at the end of the day, I'm glad I was able to do what I was supposed to do.

**When I** was in sixth grade, I'd fallen out of a tree and fractured both of my legs. I had played football, and I was obviously pretty gifted at it. But after I fell, they had to put pins and plates in my ankles. The doctor said I needed to do something else. I started playing saxophone in the band.

**My daughter** Dakota is 9. I have a stepson, Michael, who's 13. Gina, my wife, and I have a boy, Daniel Robert. Baby Danimal is a truck. He's lean-built. A big little fella.

**I was** very goal-driven, and the goal, obviously, is to go to the Super Bowl and win it. We had it within our grasp, but we didn't close the deal, especially in '86 and '87.

**It's too** simple to say, "Oh, well, our quarterback was never healthy," but I find it hard to believe that New England would've won three of the last four without Tom Brady.

**My problem** with him[1] was everybody had their own individual goals or objectives. I can't blame him for not having the same goals or objectives that I did. Every game was important, and every season is the most important. Jim had other ideas about how to go about it. He was looking at the long road, wanting a 15-year career.

**A lot** of it came from the mentality of our team. McMichael and I and Ditka, we were Cro-Magnon. I think in a way that's what made that team special. The future doesn't belong to anybody. Today is the day.

**I've got** a Hall of Fame ring and I've got a Super Bowl ring, and everybody says, "Which do you like the most?" I said, "Well, there's only 120 Hall of Fame rings in the world, but that's the only Chicago Bears Super Bowl ring there is."

1. Jim McMahon.

# Dennis McKinnon

### THEN: No. 85, wide receiver   NOW: Board member

**The thing** I'm proudest of was that I was part of a group of guys who did what they had to do, who gave Walter a chance to be in a place he should've always been.

**He was** the quintessential icon. I was humbled by his presence.

**Even today,** there's not a day that goes by that I don't think about him. I still say that this city has not honored him the way he should be. No different than the National Football League. We hope to change that.

**We would** love to be able to get the National Football League on one given Sunday that a percentage of all tickets sold in all the markets goes to the Walter Payton Fund, which is something that has never been done, not even in our own back yard.

**Having the** great Payton, we were a running team. Everybody talks about how great our defense was, but it's ironic that we led the league in time of possession, second in the league in scoring, three consecutive years I think we led the league in rushing, which means the defense was definitely rested.

**Our offense,** we never wanted to sit on the bench. We wanted to stand and see what quarterback would get knocked out. There was always a bounty on every quarterback.

**We were** so disappointed that we didn't get the Dolphins. We never believed the Patriots had a prayer anyway.

**Opening lineup.** We're in the tunnel. They're doing the introductions, and they said, "No. 85, from Florida State, Dennis McKinnon." Here I am, in my third year in the league, a free-agent walk-on, has a chance to start at a place I never thought I would be. It's remarkable when you look back on it.

**Yeah, I** complained. Yeah, I was screaming, "Willie's not open. I am. Throw me the ball. What do I have to do? Who else do I have to knock out?"

**The McKinnon** payoff? At a time where if you were really good at returning kicks, teams didn't kick it to you. A majority of our guys who were on special teams weren't making a whole lot of money. I wanted to insure my safety. I would always tell whoever makes the block that springs me, there's $5,000 or $10,000 for you.

**Here's a** guy in my first year I couldn't stand.[1] I got yelled at every single practice as a rookie. He had me learning three different positions—flanker, split end, tight end. Then I had veteran players tell me the wrong plays because they didn't want to practice. I was frustrated, frustrated, frustrated. Then I realized that he saw something in me that some people didn't see.

**Most of** the boards I sit on are prevalent to raising money for kids to go to school, because I knew how important scholarships were to me. I'm a product of how important education is.

**We did** something so special to this town because we played for a city. We didn't just play for the Bears or for the McCaskeys. We played for the city of Chicago. For every Bear fan who got off a plane in any city, they were proud to be from Chicago.

1. Mike Ditka.

# Otis Wilson

**THEN:** No. 55, linebacker
**NOW:** Camp leader

**We had** the '80s, and Michael had the '90s.

**When you** say "showmen," we were just a crazy bunch of guys with great personalities, but when it was time to work, we went to work.

**With Buddy** Ryan doing some of the things he did and Mike being vocal, hey, everybody was crazy.

**One thing** Buddy said: "If you don't know what you're doing, you'll be standing over here by me."

**I couldn't** stand him at first. No. 1, he wouldn't call us by our names. And he was on us so hard. But he wanted you to understand what was really going on. By my second year, it clicked in my head. I understood the total picture, and it made me a better player.

**It sounded** stupid.[1] It sounded cocky. But, hey, we did it. We put ourselves out there in front of the bullet and made it happen.

**Willie Gault** put that together, and Harold Washington was in office. They were trying to come up with an idea to raise money for various charities. That was the whole focus. It wasn't that we were trying to relate it to football. We were trying to raise money for charity. But it just turned out that way.

**Singletary, an** intense, smart individual. Hard-nosed. Almost like a coach on the field. Dedicated. Watching him study and understand the game helped me as well.

**Playing with** Wilber, I called him "Pit Bull," because he got on you and don't let you go.

**Dave Duerson** and I, when we played, we'd get a little excited, a little carried away sometimes. We were just saying, "We're like a pack of dogs out here." We just started barking, and that's how it all started, believe it or not. I wish I could've put a patent on it. I'd be Bill Gates.

**You couldn't** double-team anyone on that line. If you double-team Richard, Hampton and McMichael would take your head off.

**We saw** something in everybody's eyes.

**We were** coming, and they were like, "Oh, Lord, here they come again."

**The fans** have always been great here in Chicago. Twenty years later, they can still name every player on that team. It's recognized, it's appreciated, and their support's always been great.

**The wildest** thing I wore? A thong on the beach in Hawaii.

**My memorable** stuff is happening now. No. 1, I do my football camp. It's called ASC—Athletic Sports Camp. We're at Illinois Benedictine. And my health and fitness program, which is called 55 Alive, and I'm working with kids. That's giving back to the community. Going into these communities, working with these young kids, giving them a foundation so they can understand and make good life choices. It's a blessing.

**All of** us are still working. All of us are still successful. You got what you got, and you're still getting. Twenty years later, I'm still getting.

**It's a** brutal sport. You see this guy going into his fifth year, and this guy coming out of college is 21. I only have to pay him $20,000. I have to pay you a million. Which one do you think they're going to pay? You've got to look at all these things, kid. Don't go in there stupid.

**Ed McCaskey** used to always tell me, "Otis, are you saving your money?" I'd say, "Yes, I'm saving my money. I'm saving for a rainy day. I'm investing it wisely." Then I'm saying in my mind, "Because I'm not getting enough of it."

1. "The Super Bowl Shuffle."

# Jim McMahon

## THEN: No. 9, quarterback    NOW: Bon vivant

**It amazes** me that we didn't win four of them. We lost 11 games in four years and only won one Super Bowl.

**I haven't** watched a game in seven years. I was a player, that's it.

**Like I** told Ditka years ago, "I don't care what you call, I just want the freedom when I get to the line of scrimmage, if it's not a good play, to get out of it." That's what these guys don't do now. Nobody wants to take it on their shoulders to say, "I'm not going to call that play. It's not going to work." They can just go in the locker room after the game and go, "Well, the coach called it." They don't want to take any heat. That's another reason I don't watch it. A bunch of robots.

**We had** our moments. He was a tough coach. Had we played together, I think he would've understood me a little bit better, had he been in my huddle. I think he finally figured out that I knew what I was doing.

**I thought** the best player I ever played against was Wilber Marshall, and that was every day in practice until he went to the Redskins.

**I think** the people who meet me and spend some time with me know that I'm not the guy they see in the papers.

**The kid** I met at the Elway tournament. He's a 22-year-old kid, just got back from Iraq. He's in the Army and he got his calf blown off. They had to amputate his leg. He caddied for me all week in Denver. He amazed me. Kid had a great attitude.

**I said,** "What happened?" He said, "We were out on patrol, got ambushed." He said, "I thought I just took some shrapnel in my leg, and I looked down and my leg is gone." I said, "What'd you do?" He said, "We were in a firefight. I kept firing." He said he got three of them after they got him. That impressed me.

**Golf, 185** days last year I was on the road. One-day, two-day events.

**I'm 0-for-2.**[1] Never again.

**The fans** are about the same—maybe a little more rabid in Green Bay, because there's nothing else to do, other than ice-fish, and I didn't do that.

**They've always** treated me well,[2] even when I came back in a Green Bay Packers uniform. I got cheered. That's why I'm still living in Chicago. Been there 22 years, probably another five until my youngest gets out of high school, then I'm probably getting out of town. Somewhere warm, man. I'm getting tired of the cold.

**Money is** dwindling out of my account with two kids in college.

**I've been** very fortunate that all my kids have been great. No trouble. That's all I was ever in when I was a kid. They're much easier on me than I was on my folks, I'll tell you that.

**I'd never** had anything like that happen to me before.[3] Like I told the cop and the judge, I think someone put something in one of my drinks. You know, that's not the first time I've had a drink. I've never been in a car not knowing I was in a car. I had no idea I was even driving. That's pretty scary to drive 30 miles the wrong way and not know you're in a car.

**I'm on** probation. Otherwise I'd be drinking a beer now. I won't drink hard liquor anymore.

**Played with** a lot of great people. That's what I remember—guys I played with, friends I made in the league. I just had a good time.

1. In restaurants carrying his name.
2. Bears fans.
3. His arrest for drunken driving in Florida in 2003.

# Willie Gault

THEN: No. 83, wide receiver
NOW: Actor, screenwriter

**"The Super Bowl Shuffle"** came about when I was doing another video with Sister Sledge. From that, the producer of that video, Linda Clifford, we started talking and we said we should do a Bears video.

**I think** it was a really gutsy thing that we did. It was revolutionary. Historic. I think it was part of who we were. It fit us perfectly because we were a team that was very confident.

**46-10.** "The Super Bowl Shuffle." Walter Payton. The Fridge. McMahon's headband. Richard Dent, MVP. Amazing defense. It's a magical moment that will never be lived again. So you look at those moments and you cherish them.

**We had** people coming from Russia, Germany, Japan, everywhere, watching our practice. We were arguably one of the most popular teams in the history of the NFL.

**I don't** think there was a better coach for our team that year. I think Mike exemplified what the Bears were all about—the way he played, his tenacity. That's the same way he coached.

**Buddy Ryan,** same thing.

**Walter was** a mentor. When I first came to camp as a rookie, he was one of the first persons to greet me. He gave me a hug and almost squeezed the breath out of me.

**See, here's** the thing with me: I know who I am. I don't really need someone to validate me to tell me who I am. I know who I am.

**Steve McMichael** just wrote a book and said some things that weren't very nice, but I don't really care, because it's Steve's opinion. In my book, Steve's opinion doesn't make me walk or talk every day. My opinion of myself does.

**I would** go into Mayor Washington's office and we would talk about the city, life, people, the Bears and all that. We had a special relationship.

**My mom** and dad were probably some of my best friends. They were friends, but yet they were disciplinarians. They taught me right from wrong. They let me make decisions in my life very early. But they gave me tools to make those decisions.

**I had** good friends and good enemies. Good enemies are the ones who tell you you're not going to do anything or be anything, and in your mind you go, "I'll prove it."

**I knew** that I was the fastest guy on the field.

**I ran** a 4.2 40 not too long ago.

**I took** more hits than anybody could imagine. I have all my catches on one reel—catches and being thrown to, all of it—and I got hit a lot. It's a contact sport. People think I didn't like it, but the object of a receiver is not to get hit. You want to try to catch the ball and try to make a touchdown.

**The ballet** was an opportunity to help save the Chicago City Ballet, which I'd never done before, but I thought it would be worthwhile saving.

**I was** in "The Pretender" for three years. I had a recurring role. Then several episodes of "The West Wing" and a lot of other episodic television things.

**I'm writing** a screenplay of a book I've adapted and a couple of TV shows I created that I'm trying to get on the air.

**I'm friendly** with Denzel Washington. His wife and my wife had babies at the same time in the same hospital.

**If I** live my life based on opinions and what people say and think, then I would be a really sad person.

**Be your** own man. Be a leader, not a follower. That's the main thing.

# Gary Fencik

**THEN:** No. 45, safety
**NOW:** Securities executive

**Ditka said** that if we ever won the Super Bowl, people would remember you forever. I guess we're in the forever stage.

**I remember** the first time we met Mike in an off-season camp in Phoenix. He basically told us for the first time—and this was my third head coach with the Bears—that our goal wasn't just to get to the Super Bowl, but it was to win it.

**But he** said that "half of you won't be there when we get there." If you look at the roster, there was a two-thirds turnover from the time he gave that speech to the time we won it.

**I give** Mike a lot of credit because who today would come in as a head coach inheriting a defensive coordinator who was hired by the president/founder of the club? That was a delicate situation. I don't think Buddy[1] did anything to make that easier.

**I'm a huge** fan of Buddy's. It was an honor to play in that defense.

**People always** talk about how coaches discipline teams. Great teams discipline themselves.

**Walter Payton** was such a leader that if you had people who came in and thought they were the next big thing, not that Walter said anything, but just by the way he conducted himself, I think he humbled you into appreciating what he did.

**I think** of the great moments being beating Dallas 44-0, which for me was the first time that I had ever beaten the Cowboys in any preseason, regular season or postseason game. I was in my 10th year.

**I felt** pretty good coming off the field after their field goal[2], but there was something up on the scoreboard that basically said that 19 out of 20 teams that score first win. And I went from feeling pretty good to feeling like a Chicagoan.

**Growing up** in Chicago, you can remember every good moment in sports because there have been so few.

**My dad** was a basketball coach. I loved hoops. My mom attended all of my sporting events

for myself and all of my brothers and sisters, and knitted. So we had a lot of knitted sweaters when we were growing up.

**My dad** was an assistant principal of a high school, so I think that probably speaks for itself what the academic expectations were.

**I knew** I wanted to enjoy football, but I was looking for something bigger, and Yale is a pretty impressive place when you visit it.

**I ran** with the bulls in Pamplona. That was stupid. I did it a few weeks before training camp. As I was running for my life, I was thinking, "This isn't too smart to do."

**I'm really** glad I went to business school at Northwestern. My first two classes were accounting and statistics, and we're coming back from beating the Raiders, and I'm

studying for a final the next day, and everybody else is drinking beer and playing cards. I'm like, "Why did I start business school during the football season?"

**A lot** of people still continue to confuse Doug[3] and I. I had someone call me Doug Fencik. I don't even shake my head anymore. I just recognize the compliment.

**I work** for a money-management firm based in Chicago with an office in London.

**Best piece** of advice I ever got was: Make sure the door you go into has two doors going out.

1. Buddy Ryan.
2. When New England took a 3-0 lead in Super Bowl XX.
3. Doug Plank.

# Richard Dent

THEN: No. 95, defensive end   NOW: Executive

**The championship** game with the Rams, seeing the snow coming down, the guys are happy because you know you're going to the Super Bowl. To be at home and feel the enjoyment that was taking place was awesome.

**I'm sure** they[1] knew it was over before they got there.

**In certain** formations and certain things they would get into, myself or Mike[2] or Hampton would call that play out, and you'd see their guys looking at each other.

**I think** Mike[3] always kept us on the edge. He had ways of getting us ready.

**Some of** the things, we didn't see eye to eye on—some of the ways in trying to motivate me that I didn't appreciate. But outside of that, we had a good time.

**Buddy put** the game in our hands. He put the game plan in our hands. You don't see that much today. You see it maybe with Peyton Manning. You see it mostly on the offensive side. You don't see it on the defensive side.

**You think** about things like not letting teams score, negative yards at halftime—you just don't see that. Some of the things we did, you just don't see. And the point of it was that you shared some things with some guys that were very rare.

**The way** people look at us and this particular team—how much we won, how well we played, how well we entertained people—

people think we won three, four Super Bowls. We had that caliber of team. We tampered with the quarterback position a lot.

**I thought** we should've won more Super Bowls. We lost a couple opportunities there with Flutie.

**I'm an** eighth-rounder, and when you're drafted in that position, you're there for a couple years until they find something better. In this case, they found something great.

**You're trying** to figure out a guy's weakness, and what I would do is work on his weakness. In your eyes, you think I'm taking a play off. But you don't understand the game, so you wouldn't know what I'm doing. I spend my week working on things where a guy's weak.

**At RLD** Resources, the company I run, we're into gas and electric and communications and fuel management. I manage all the gas in the Chicago Public Schools, and I've saved them quite a few million dollars.

**My mother** used to have a catering service. I did whatever she asked me to do—setting tables, cooking, washing dishes, whatever.

**I guess** when I was growing up I always wanted to be someone in my community that people looked up to. I had dreams of a Super Bowl team, Super Bowl MVP, all the things that I accomplished. Yes, I had dreams of that.

**If you** don't know how to commit yourself, then you aren't going to be anything.

**I guess** I'm a people watcher. I enjoy seeing people accomplish dreams and things of that nature. I remember meeting Venus Williams back in '87, '88. Watching people go from nowhere to get to somewhere.

**Because I** know I've kind of done the same thing. I had the chance to crawl out from under a rock, from nowhere to become something.

**I had** an uncle named "Rabbit" who was Gary Player's caddie for 20 years. I remember him back in the years talking about the people he caddied for. Golf was the first sport I went out for, but I didn't stay that long because the teacher who was teaching it was the football coach, and he was trying to make me play football, but I didn't want to play football because I was working and making money.

**I've always** had the mind frame of doing your own thing. When you work for people from the fourth grade until the 12th grade, I understand what a hard living is all about.

**If I** can bring other people along within my business and get their dreams and goals, that's what it's all about—giving back and reaching back.

1. The Patriots.
2. Singletary.
3. Ditka.

# Dave Duerson

THEN: No. 22, safety  NOW: Businessman

**My dad** is my hero. My dad's decorated—two Bronze Stars from World War II, fought in the 3rd Army Signal Corps directly under Patton. He spent a lot of his time behind enemy lines.

**So when** I went to work for Buddy Ryan, it was like a joke. Buddy Ryan and Mike Ditka couldn't intimidate me.

**Buddy certainly** had attitude, but his was self-serving. Very much so. You were either one of his guys, or you weren't. In my case, I wasn't.

**Buddy just** absolutely hated my guts. Hated my guts. I called my dad when I first got drafted and I told him, "Dad, I didn't graduate from college to go through this." My dad believes that every male child should do two years in the armed services. I tell you that as a precursor. So he says to me, "Well, it sounds to me like you're in the Army." So I said, "OK, Dad, I'll talk to you later." Short phone call.

**Every day** Buddy would tell me he was waiting for me to screw up one time. So I played through that whole season with the defensive coordinator telling me that he was rooting for me to screw up so he could get Todd[1] back.

**So I** became an All-Pro myself.

**I think** Eason[2] knew it was over the second series. Absolutely. He picked himself off the turf on each play of the first series and the second series. Their offensive line couldn't handle our guys.

**With all** the things we were doing at the line of scrimmage, we were calling out their plays before they could execute them.

**I was** projected to go to Parcells with the 10th pick in the first round. He took Terry Kinnard instead. I was talking about the importance of law school.

**It was** never just football for me. It cost me two rounds in the draft.

**My company** is Duerson Foods. We are ground-meat experts. And I have Duerson Capital Holdings, so my money goes upstream.

**I think** we should've won three Super Bowls. But they started shipping guys out.

1. Todd Bell, cornerback, who was holding out that year.
2. Patriots quarterback Tony Eason.

# Emery Moorehead

## THEN: No. 87, tight end  NOW: Realtor

**Our team,** everybody knew we were going to the Super Bowl. After we lost to the 49ers the year before in the NFC championship, Ditka made a point of saying: "Remember this. We're going to be back." Hampton I remember saying, "We're going to win the damn thing next year." Everybody came back with a purpose.

**I remember** being in the locker room and everybody being ecstatic. But it was a situation where we knew we were going to win. We expected to win. We really did.

**Ditka, I think,** was a pretty good coach. He was a great motivator. Not a great tactician, but certainly a great motivator of men. He got the best out of everybody.

**We led** the league in rushing. We led the league in time of possession. We were underrated as an offense because the defense was just phenomenal.

**He was** an iron man out there.[1] He played with pain. Throwing up in the huddle. The guy loved to play football and loved to play every down.

**Our line,** we always had a lot of good surges, trying to get out of the Fridge's way.

**I started** selling real estate with Koenig & Strey right after the Super Bowl.

**I also** have Moorehead Construction Services. I do representation for people who have a job they want to do and they need someone between them and the contractors.

**Bears fans,** most of them still think you play. It's crazy. They think you're still 30 years old or whatever. The comment most often is "You should be playing" and "They haven't had a tight end since you left."

**Having been** born and raised in Evanston, I certainly could appreciate it a little bit more than some of the other players winning the Super Bowl and how long it had been since the city had won a championship.

**My father** was a garbage man for Evanston. My mother worked at the post office for years. Just a typical family from Evanston. Blue-collar family that worked.

**Every kid** wanted to be Dick Butkus and Gale Sayers.

**Myself, always** being a die-hard Cubs fan, Ernie Banks was No. 1 over everything.

**I was** at a dinner, and Ernie was in the back telling stories and signing autographs. I waited until everybody had talked to him, and then I went up and introduced myself.

It was like I was a little kid again. I was in my 30s.

**My son**[2] is 24 and is in his third year with the Indianapolis Colts. My daughter[3] is 21 and is a (student) at Illinois. Just watching them grow up to be good people and make good decisions and have other people come back and tell you that your kid's a nice guy or what a good job you did—that's what I look at now. Because you never know. You do the best you can and you hope they act right when they're around other people, but hearing that feedback from other parents is the most rewarding thing.

1. Walter Payton.
2. Aaron.
3. Kelly.

# William Perry

THEN: No. 72, defensive tackle  NOW: Fisherman

**I moved** back home to Aiken, S.C. I'm doing a lot of fishing, and I'm really relaxing and enjoying myself. Mainly, that's it.

**I did** have a construction company and everything, but I did away with that. Me and my wife divorced, and I had that company with her daddy, and I said I'm going one way and you go the other way.

**We got** divorced about three years ago. Don't be sorry. Everything's fine.

**I wish** we could've stayed together and raised our kids as one, but she wanted to go her separate way, and she did. We have two little kids, and my two older daughters are married, and I'm a grandparent.

**Yeah, my** oldest had a daughter. I have a granddaughter.

**The grandchild**—you got me on that one. I can't barely hardly remember the kids' names.

**It's still** the same. People see me and say hello, say, "That's the Fridge." Take a picture.

**It started** in San Francisco. That's when I first ran the ball. Then on Monday night,[1] that's where it all blew up and everybody saw me and took to me, and everything happened after that.

**I was** a running back way back in the day, but you get to professional ball and you can score touchdowns and all, now it's just funny to me.

**That was** one crazy play.[2] I was supposed to go out and block on the cornerback. I went out and blocked on Everson Walls. Walter was going up the middle. I went and blocked on Walls, and we was out there talkin' for a few seconds, and I look back and everybody was on Walter. I went back into the crowd that was tackling Walter and knocked everybody off and grabbed him and pulled him into the end zone. The referee said, "You can't do that! You can't do that!" I said, "It's done now."

**I couldn't** say too much about Walter. He was a great guy, a class act, a wonderful person on and off the field. We spent plenty of time going out to his places, his clubs, played pickup basketball together.

**To me,** he was a wonderful guy, a wonderful coach, a nice person, a great all-around guy.[3] He's the one that drafted me, and I appreciated that. He's the one that gave me a chance and put me in the backfield and stuff. I still love him and appreciate him and give him the utmost respect.

**My mother** told me not to talk about people unless I can say something good about them.

**My mom** and my dad brought 12 of us up, eight brothers and four sisters. She taught us well. She passed about 15 years ago. Most of us are having a great life. Some

passed, and they had a great life. That's why I say enjoy yourself; you never know what goes on.

**Money is** nothing. You can't take it with you when you go to heaven. I use it as a tool to keep going.

**I let** them talk about it.[4] I was happy then. I'm happy now.

**That came** from Clemson. Me and the guys, we went out one night, having a couple beers, and we came back and there was an elevator in our dormitory. I was so big then and I walked through it, and a light was hanging down, and the guy behind me said, "You ain't nothing but a walking refrigerator," and that's how I got the name.

**I don't** believe in collecting anything. I just don't.

**You've got** to say the favorite moment was scoring a touchdown in the Super Bowl. That's what you work for the whole time, from peewee ball all the way through. You get the chance to score a touchdown, so I can't say no more. That was the highlight of the whole thing.

1. Against the Packers.
2. When he was in the backfield against Dallas.
3. Mike Ditka.
4. His weight.

# Ron Rivera

THEN: No. 59, linebacker
NOW: Bears defensive coordinator

**I would** love to be in a position[1] where people say, "These guys remind me of the '85 team." I would love to have that every day, every week.

**But right** now, we've got a ways to go.

**Do we** have some players who are comparable to those players on the '85 Bears? Oh, we do. I believe we do. I think Brian Urlacher is going to be comparable to Mike Singletary when we get there. I think Alex Brown, if he continues to grow, he could be comparable to Richard Dent. I think Adewale Ogunleye could be comparable to Richard.

**Jeremy Shockey,** he said, "Coach, great job. Your guys played hard." That meant more to me than anything I've read from anybody.

**The one** thing I loved about Mike Ditka is he was honest with you.

**One of** the first things that happened to me in 1984 was coach Ditka always made it a point that the rookies were introduced to Mrs. McCaskey, to Virginia, and she gave us the autobiography "Halas By Halas." Ed, as ever, was joking, but I thought he was serious when he said, "I hope you guys enjoy the book, and by the way there's going to be a test on this book." So I read the book.

**Buddy was** one of those guys that tore you down, broke you down, beat you up to build you up. He loved you and you learned to love him.

**Buddy said,** "You're slower than Buffone." Once I found out who Doug Buffone was, I was really hurt.

**Guys were** sniffling and crying.[2] Real quiet. Then all of a sudden, out of nowhere, McMichael goes, "What a bunch of crybabies. We're getting ready to play the most important game of our lives, and all you guys can do is whine about this?" And he grabs a chair and throws it across the room, and it sticks in the chalkboard.

**If we'd** have played them that night, we'd have beaten them 100-0.

**Walter Payton.** As large an individual as he was in terms of the whole scope and magnitude of being an NFL player, he was a good person.

**I put** it away for a while.[3] Broke it out, we beat Green Bay, then I put it away.

**I was** telling a group of kids one time, "Everybody talks about the money, the jewelry. That doesn't mean anything. What means something are the people in the room that you do these things with. That's what's special. Someday my son's going to inherit this ring, but it won't have the same value to him that it has to me."

**I was** an Army brat.

**When I** was growing up in the military, there was a rank system, a class system. There wasn't a black or white.

**When we** moved back to the United States from Panama ... I was stunned by the racism. I played flag football in junior high. We had a lot of black kids on our team, and one of the guys got cut, and this white kid from this small town looked and said, "Y'all bleed red blood too?" I was shocked. I guess I was naive.

1. As defensive coordinator of the Bears.
2. The night before the Super Bowl when Buddy Ryan told the defense he would be leaving the Bears after that game.
3. His Super Bowl ring.

# Keith Van Horne

## THEN: No. 78, offensive tackle  NOW: Investor

**That year** was the highlight of my football career and the low point of my personal life.

**My dad** passed away on the 28th of December. The fact that we still had to play was probably a good thing for me because I could just focus on that, because I was in another world.

**The last** years of his life, we kind of got close and took it to a different level.

**That generation,** I think you know what I'm talking about, kept things in. But it got to the point when I went to college that that started changing. I was on my own. I had some independence, could say yes or no to any advice he might give me. But you start realizing how smart your parents are because you start experiencing things they talked to you about when you thought they don't know what they're talking about, and then you find out, well, I guess they actually did.

**Once the** game was over, I went right to the locker room and started grieving. It was a huge relief to get it over with.

**I miss** him still. He was a good man.

**Here's the** second part: Andy Frederick, who was our backup at tackle, got hurt in pregame warmups, so Jimbo Covert and I looked at each other and said, "Oh, God. We don't have anyone to replace us." I had to play the whole game.

**Shame on** us. I think Dan Hampton said that—shame on us for not going back—and he's right.

**Our defense** developed into probably the best defense that ever played. Certainly in the top two or three ever.

**It was** fun watching them. You could see the fear in the eyes of opposing offenses, the quarterbacks especially.

**People talk** about our defense all the time, and rightfully so. But we led the league in time of possession, led the league in scoring, led the league in rushing. So we were able to do some stuff too.

**Part of** the reason we were able to run the ball so well is we had to practice against those guys. And our practices were not like I think they practice today. We had Ditka, so we were out there hitting each other.

**He[1] knew** football. He could come out and audible or change the play that was sent in if he didn't like it, which didn't always go over so well with Ditka. But I think Jim had a

better grasp of it than Ed Hughes[2] and Mike Ditka, let me tell you.

**Up in** Green Bay when he[3] went in, he ran right over me and just nailed me in the back. I scored as well.

**Walter was** the real deal. He was the workhorse. I've been very blessed, very honored. I blocked for Charlie White and Marcus Allen in college. They both won a Heisman

Trophy. Then I got to come to Chicago and got to block for the greatest all-around running back that ever played, in my opinion.

**I'm proud** and honored to be a part of Chicago history.

1. Jim McMahon.
2. Offensive coordinator.
3. William "The Refrigerator" Perry.

# Steve McMichael

## THEN: No. 76, defensive tackle NOW: Author

**This thing** isn't going to die out, this '85 Bears thing, baby. We were entertainers, you understand? We were entertainers as well as a great football team. That's why everybody remembers us in the pantheon of pro football. We could've been the team of the decade if McMahon had stayed healthy. But he didn't.

**I knew** there was going to be something special downtown when we left the airport and all the exits from O'Hare to downtown were blocked off. There was no traffic. There was no traffic even waiting to come on where it was blocked off. So I knew everybody was downtown.

**Mike Ditka** brought the "Monsters of the Midway" back to Chicago. They'd been gone since Dick Butkus. That's why he's beloved.

**Listen, baby,** we were vicious. That's the Cro-Magnon that Hampton talked about, and teams were scared to come in here and play us.

**I'm not** talking about scared whether they were going to win or lose. I'm talking about scared if they were going to get out of the game walking or on a stretcher.

**When Wilber** Marshall hit Joe Ferguson in Detroit, ooohhh, my goodness. You can't do it anymore, but it was legal back then. Ferguson was out before he hit the ground, and how I knew he was out was Richard Dent, like a referee in boxing, he picked up Ferguson's arm and let it go and it just flopped back down.

**I think** we put out six starting quarterbacks that year.

**They gave** me the paper that we wanted Halas to keep Buddy no matter who the coach was, and I signed it, even though Buddy wasn't playing me yet. That's the kind of respect I had for him. I wanted him to stick around long enough for him to put me in the game and play me. Then I knew I'd done something. I was proud of myself when that happened.

**One of** the best games I played in pro football was that year against the San Francisco 49ers in Candlestick Park. I got a game ball and we beat them 26-10. That's when I knew we were going to win the Super Bowl, because they were the defending world champions, they were there in all their glory, they didn't have any injuries, it was in their house, and we whipped their (butts).

**Buddy would** give us a little speech before the game and walk out of the meeting, and Dale Haupt, the defensive line coach, would run the projector and we'd watch one more reel of film. Well, the night before the Super Bowl, Buddy got up in front of us, and the last thing he said before he walked out of the room was, "No matter what happens, you guys will always be my heroes." I knew he was gone. Tears in his eyes, you understand?

**After he** walked out and closed the door, I stood up, picked up the metal chair that was under me, those folding chairs, and threw it into the blackboard that was right in front of me. It was like a movie special effect. I was trying to shatter the board. All four legs impaled the thing and just hung there. The room erupted.

**That's when** Hampton clubbed the projector and said, "This meeting's over." And we all filed out yelling and screaming.

**That fever** pitch that started right there kind of carried through till about halftime, and we'd already blown the game out.

**I might** not ever be in the Hall of Fame, but there's guys in there that are, and I've whipped their (butts).

**In every** Shakespearean tragedy, there's some comic relief, and that's what William Perry was for us.

**The book** is called "Tales from the Chicago Bears Sidelines," by Steve McMichael, of course. It's a chronicle of my life in football.

**"Mongo" I** got from the Bears' practices and fighting all the time.

**You know** the Bam Bam character from the Flintstones carrying the club around and beating the (heck) out of everything? That was me. In the book, I talk about being a bouncer in a strip joint, and when I cruised the parking lot, I had a bat in my hand, so I did look just like Bam Bam.

**I won** a local Emmy doing TV in Chicago, you kidding me? It wasn't with Mark Giangreco.[1] We had the No. 1-rated show. But it was me and Bruce Wolf my last year in town on Fox. You don't remember that, do you?

**You know** why most wrestlers have long hair and it's flowing? It sells better when you sell the fake punch.

**All-Pro,** Super Bowl champion, Monster of the Midway. That's the triple crown, baby.

1. Then on WMAQ-Ch. 5.

# Leslie Frazier

THEN: No. 21, cornerback   NOW: Defensive coach, Colts

**I came** in town for the first time in a while for the Bears convention, and I could not believe the way the fans treated myself and the other guys who played in the Super Bowl. It was almost like we just won it this past February.

**When we** were walking off the field at halftime and they were playing "The Super Bowl Shuffle," it was almost like it was a home field for us.

**As far** as I'm concerned, the greatest running back ever.[1] But a great human being who really tried to reach out to me and other young players and tried to be a good example.

**The scheme** that we ran was so unique at the time. It took a lot of pressure off our defensive backs. People thought we were under a lot of pressure because we played so much man and we blitzed so much, but he[2] would tell us, "Just cover them an extra second, Leslie, and we'll get there," and boy, we usually got there.

**I don't** think I would have that Super Bowl ring if not for him.[3] Without question. When he came in, I don't know if we really understood what it took to win in the National Football League, the sacrifice that was necessary, the importance of teamwork. He instilled that toughness that we needed to get over the hump.

**Next to** us winning a Super Bowl and meeting some of the guys I met, that period of time at Trinity College was probably the greatest period of my life. To come in there and start a football program at 28 years of age and be an African-American head coach at a Christian college was a great time.

**I'll be** working with the secondary with Indianapolis. My title is senior defensive assistant. It keeps me in the mix, and it keeps me with a real good football team.

**The birth** of my kids and the lady I married—those are experiences I wouldn't change for anything in the world.

1. Walter Payton.
2. Buddy Ryan.
3. Mike Ditka.

# Tom Thayer

THEN: No. 57, guard
NOW: Surfer

**It starts** with Joliet Catholic and wanting to play football there, playing college football somewhere, and then always shooting for the stars, and shooting for the stars was the NFL, and the Bears were always a dream situation.

**The day** we were announcing my USFL contract,[1] it was the same day as the NFL draft, and here I am, sitting in a room with George Allen, signing a contract so I can stay in Chicago, and after that announcement I drive home and pull into my driveway, and my sister says, "Jim Finks is on the phone. The Bears just drafted you."

**I kind** of felt like I blew the opportunity to live out every childhood dream in playing for your hometown team. But on the positive end of it, I signed a three-year contract, and the Bears had my rights for four years.

**The best** thing about that year[2] was losing the coin toss and letting the defense go on the field first. Those guys usually set the tone.

**Ditka was** great because he motivated by fear of losing your job. I think if you have any pride or any passion for the game of football, that's one of the best motivations you can have.

**Walter was** the toughest man I've ever known. He was physically fit and tough. If you go back and look at Walter's football helmet, he wore the old suspension helmet—the one that just has the belt around your head, the one that doesn't have that sophisticated pad system that they have today—and he never missed a game with a head injury. He never left a game because he had a concussion.

**Every time** I think of Fridge, I smile.

**I think** Keith Van Horne was as smart about our offense as our quarterbacks were.

**Super Bowl** XX, I was so young in my NFL career that I expected it to happen again.

**You hear** people talk about, "Oh, you should've won it two or three more times." Maybe not, but at least one more time.

**For me,** as an ex-Bear and as a Chicago resident, I get frustrated going to opponents'

stadiums and talking to different people involved with different teams, and they don't have that fear of the Bears coming. There's no respect for the Bears' swagger.

**I think** it's my Type-A personality. It's the best thing I've ever done since I quit playing football[3]. When you pull up to the ocean and you look out and you see that the surf is 10 feet, that puts the same nervousness in your stomach that you felt before kickoff. I think that's healthy for me.

**My mom** and dad are on their 54th year of marriage, and my brothers and sisters all get together and get along, and I think a lot of that has to do with the fact that we all got to follow football for so long together.

**My dad** worked 43 years of his life for Commonwealth Edison. He worked outdoors every day of his life.

**My first** contract in the USFL, my dad said, "You're going to make in three years what it's taken me 34."

**My mom** and my brother run the restaurant, Thayer Brothers Deli and Grill in Joliet. You go in there and see my mom. She makes everything homemade.

**What am** I proudest of? Man, it sounds corny, but it's being able to experience everything in my professional life with my family.

1. With the Chicago Blitz.
2. The 1985 regular season.
3. Surfing in Hawaii.

# Jay Hilgenberg

THEN: No. 63, center  NOW: Land developer

**We accepted** it as an offensive line that if we win, all the credit's going to go someplace else, but if we lose, it's going to come at us.

**We had** a great defense, no doubt about it. The week of practice I'd have at Lake Forest a lot of times was harder than games.

**But if** you look at that season, the early games, teams were scoring some points on us. It took a few games for the defense to start shutting it down, but once they did, they were devastating to offenses.

**The nice** thing about Ditka is you always knew where you stood.

**Head coaches,** that's their role: They're supposed to yell and scream and do all that.

**When Ditka** came in, he got rid of guys who were just happy being professional football players. He wanted professional football players who wanted to win. He changed the whole culture.

**When he**[1] was healthy, I tell you, he was into football more than anybody there was. He loved football. He was very smart at it.

**It was** always nice to read the papers during training camp to see what was going on with him and Ditka. I remember being mad at Jim a couple times because all he was doing was getting Mike angry, and he'd take it out on us all the time.

**When we** went up to Lambeau and played the Packers, that was during the time where the quarterback didn't have to run a play if the crowd was too loud. We were on the 1-yard line going in, and McMahon was taunting the Packer fans, being really bru-

tal. They were too loud, so he wasn't going to run the play. He was just taunting the Packer fans up there. Now, this is after the Monday night game, and they all know Fridge is going to get the ball. But this was the one where they faked the run to Fridge and he went into the end zone and caught the pass for a touchdown. Just to hear Lambeau Field being so loud and McMahon's being difficult, and then hearing the quiet after Fridge caught a touchdown pass, we were just laughing so hard out there.

**Walter was** the greatest.

**I remember** the first play I was ever in on. We were going against a 3-4 defense. The nose guard threw me off, and Walter was running through the right tackle hole. I started getting back up on my feet, and I looked behind me. Remember watching as a kid the high step that Walter would do? It was just like I was a little kid watching him high-step right at me. I tried to get out of his way, but I just catch his knee with my shoulder, and he goes down. I thought, "Man, my first play in the NFL, and I tackle Walter Payton." Walter goes, "Next time, just lay on the ground."

**I remember** Willie Gault on the plane[2] asking me if I wanted to be in "The Super Bowl Shuffle." I said no. I didn't want any part of that. I said, "Are you kidding me? We just got beat on national TV, and now we're going to go sing about being in the Super Bowl? Come on."

**I was** born in Iowa City in University Hospital, so I was a Hawkeye from Day One. My father was coaching at Iowa at the time. My dad grew up in Iowa, went to the University of Iowa and in 1953 was a first-team All-American.

**My older** brother Jim was first-team All-Big Ten and a two-time captain of Iowa. When he was a senior, I was a freshman at Iowa. Then when I was a senior, Joel was a freshman at Iowa. Joel went on to play 10 years with the Saints. We were all centers.

**My uncle** Wally was an All-American football player at Iowa and played for the Vikings. He started four Super Bowls with the Vikings.

**I was** working out at home in the off-season and I felt the pain.[3] They ran a test and found a blockage in my heart. I was a pretty lucky guy.

**My daughter,** Mara. Being a dad. That's really my main thing. I went through a divorce in '91, '92.

**I'm developing** a piece of property in Kenosha, Wis., a golf course community called The Club at Strawberry Creek.

**I remember** my uncle and his advice for a football game. He'd always tell me, "Hey, you remember, first play of the game, no matter what it is, you just hit the guy in the face as hard as you can." You set the tone with the guy.

1. Jim McMahon.
2. After the Monday night loss in Miami.
3. In April 1994, which prompted his retirement.

# Thomas Sanders

## THEN: No. 20, running back  NOW: Father

**I can't** begin to understand why there's still a big, big interest in that '85 team. It's been 20 years. You'd think it would've died out. But it seems to be as huge as it was back then, which is great.

**The biggest** thing for me was after the game, coming back home to Chicago and seeing the fans. The ticker-tape parade. I'd never seen anything like that in my life.

**No. 1, you're** playing with the greatest running back ever. You're talking to him on a regular basis every day. You're lining up against Mike Singletary and Dan Hampton and all these guys in practice. At that time,

it didn't resonate a whole lot, but now I look back at it like, "Man, I was practicing against some of the greatest guys who ever played the game."

**I liked** Mike.[1] I liked his style. He didn't bite his tongue about what he wanted from you. He came straight out and told you. I respect that a lot more than somebody who wouldn't say anything but would say everything behind your back.

**To be** honest with you, my first year I didn't like being in the huddle with him.[2] Because I knew he was going to change the play.

**Down in** Miami, I think that was our wakeup

call. Things were going so well up until that point, I honestly believe that had we not lost that game, we probably wouldn't have gone to the Super Bowl.

**I think** it got people to realizing that we can be beat and we can overlook other teams. I think it brought us back down to a level where we really had to focus more.

**My most** memorable experience away from football? I would say it's something when we were growing up. My dad used to always take us to different places, and we'd always go to San Antonio to the zoo. We'd all pile into the back of the pickup truck—me, my brothers and sisters and cousins—and just go and have fun and be kids. I'm amazed that I even remember this stuff because it's such a long time ago, but to me, that's what life is about—family and being part of a group and having fun.

1. Ditka.
2. Jim McMahon.

# Kevin Butler

**THEN:** No. 6, kicker
**NOW:** Group sales exec

**Steve Kazor** picked me up at the airport and we walked up to Halas Hall, and the first guy that walked up to me was Buddy Ryan. He goes, "Hey, Steve, who's this?" Steve says, "This is Kevin Butler." Buddy looked at me and said, "Oh, God, we wasted a pick on him."

**All of** a sudden I get a hand on my shoulder, and it was Ditka. Mike's like, "Hey, don't listen to this guy. Come with me."

**If you** didn't know where you stood with Mike, all you had to do was read the paper.

**I remember** my first meeting and sitting next to Mike Hartenstine and thinking, this guy's probably killed people. He had that demeanor—stone face. As I got to know Mike, there probably wasn't a nicer guy on the team.

**The first** mini-camp, I go up there after I'm drafted. I'm engaged to be married Jan. 25. I walk out of that meeting, I get on the phone to Cathy and I say, "Hey, we've got to change our wedding." She's like, "My God, you've been up there four hours and you've already met somebody." I'm like, "No, I'm going to make the team and we're going to the Super Bowl."

**First of all,** I hear "Butt-head." That's my name for the rest of my life. I enjoy it. Every day in the mail, I'm still signing football cards.

**Bear fans,** they're true and blue. They've been through some lean years in the past. Until they carry the Lombardi Trophy off, we'll still be their favorite kids.

**The first** thing that comes to my mind: I did contribute to that Super Bowl season.

**Two games:** San Francisco and the New York Jets. I hit four field goals in each game. The Jets was a tighter game than the Frisco game, but the Frisco game was a big game for me because the year before, that's where the Bears' season came to a halt in the NFC championship game. It was a big hump for us. To go out there and to make four field goals and to contribute to the win gave my teammates a lot of confidence in me.

**You get** into the first playoff game that year, and it's the famous Landeta miss.[1] I'm thanking the Lord Landeta missed then because people forget I missed three that game.

**I made** three in the Super Bowl. That was big momentum for us.

**The one** thing the guys dug about me is that in 11 years, I never had a kickoff returned on me. I would get grief sometimes that I wasn't kicking the ball out of the end zone the way I did in college. If the other 10 guys aren't making the tackle, well, I'm going to make it. One year I was second in special-teams tackles with 11 solos.

**PGI is** an experiential marketing company.

I head up our automotive group sales. We do auto shows and ride-and-drive programs.

**I've got** a Super Bowl ring and trophy I love that's a great showpiece, and they can never take it away. But what football gave to me and Cathy, and what the Bears gave to me, is a tremendous head start in life. I'm 42 and the kids—Scarlett, Drew and Savannah—are 17, 16 and 13 years old. There's not a big disconnect.

**Hey, give** me my health and give me my family, and I can get through anything.

1. Giants punter Sean Landeta whiffing on a punt that the Bears turned into a touchdown.

# Shaun Gayle

THEN: No. 23, defensive back  NOW: Author

**The one** thing that stands out for me—and it sounds strange—it was the coin toss.

**We had** the chance to call the toss, and it was Walter's time to call it in the air, which he didn't. The coin hit the ground before he called it, and they just complained about the toss to start the game off. I thought, "OK, here we go."

**What I** think separates Mike from those great coaches is the guy coached the game like he played. When the guy tells you in his unique way how poorly you've done something, your response is, "You know, I've got to listen to this guy, because he's been there, he's done it."

**I think** Buddy's forte—and this is so different these days—Buddy could line everybody up on the defense and go down the line and tell each guy what he did the best, and then he found a way to put you in that position to do what you did best.

**In my** experience, in the defensive huddle, if you screwed a play up and got back into the huddle with the guys, you were held accountable.

**I guess** one thing that really stands out for me is a situation we had in Dallas, where we go in to play Ditka's old team, and Tom Landry, and you could actually feel not just tension, but you really understood what was on the line. It wasn't just a game. At the time they were still considered somewhat "America's Team." You could feel the relationship on a level of respect between Landry and Ditka, and with all those things together the night before the game, you would expect a fire-and-brimstone talk by Ditka to go out and get this thing done because of all the things I just explained.

**But completely** out of character, the night before the game, Ditka puts on a videotape of a comedian. I forget the guy's name, but he had this skit he would do about football, and it was pretty funny. All Mike said that night was, "You know what? If you don't know it by now, then you're not going to know it by us talking about it."

**I've got** to tell you, that whole year after the midway point, when teams came out, you could see that some were defeated before they even snapped the ball.

**At the** time, I really didn't understand how brash it was for us to do that.[1] I didn't even equate the fact that we were singing a song about the Super Bowl and we hadn't even gotten to the playoffs yet.

**We wanted** the Dolphins to win that playoff game and have that rematch in the Super Bowl.

**The martial** art that I'm involved in is called kendo, where I am a third-degree black belt.

**When I** began writing those books,[2] I did not have the first clue that they would turn out to be as popular or get as much recognition as me playing for a professional team. I'm considering getting a few more books out.

**I got** a call from Oliver Stone's people to audition for the movie "Any Given Sunday." I promptly lost the role to LL Cool J. His name is bigger in the industry than mine.

**The main** thing about my parents: Everything started with school. I had to do well in school.

**Never do** anything in victory that you would not do in defeat.

**At the** end of the day, when all is said and done and they're throwing dirt on that hole that they're going to put us all in sooner or later, it's going to come down to how you treated people, how you handled situations. That will be the legacy that you leave behind.

1. Shoot "The Super Bowl Shuffle" video.
2. The "Shaun Gayle's Sports Tales" series.

# Buddy Ryan

THEN: Defensive coordinator NOW: Horse owner and farmer

**I told** them regardless of what happened, they'd always be my heroes, and walked out.[1] They all were crying and yelling. It was a very emotional thing.

**I never** planned much of anything like that. I found it works better if you have the feeling, you know?

**Being carried** off the field in the Super Bowl in New Orleans. That's a great honor that your players carried you off after the game. It's never been done to an assistant coach before or since.

**I don't** have anything to tell you about Mike Ditka.

**I don't** have feelings either way.

**Mr. Halas** gave me the job a month before he hired Ditka and told me to hire my coaches.

**A dumb** player gets you beat, and a guy that's scared will get you beat. You have to have intelligence and toughness.

**The players** executed, and they just scared people.

**I think** there was actually some fear. People laugh when you say "NFL" and have somebody scared. Well, believe me, we had them scared.

**When they** started out as rooks, they were numbers. As they got up and played well, I started calling them by name.

**If you** remember, Mike Singletary and Todd Bell and Al Harris all held out that year. I

spent the whole off-season begging them to sign up. Singletary did, but the other two didn't come into the fold, so they didn't get a Super Bowl ring.

**Moments that** year? Oh, they were all great. Dominated in the Super Bowl the way we did.

**We'd always** score the first 10 points of the game on defense and then give the offense the ball on the plus-40.

**He[2] and** I own some horses together, and he's kind of a country guy. Great player.

**If something** broke down, he'd jump the pattern.[3] He's a super-smart guy. To play our defense, you had to be smart, and you had to be tough. Gary qualified both ways.

**They wanted** me to play a three-man line, so they went out and got a nose tackle, so they thought.[4] But he could only play a couple plays, and then he had to rest.

**I used** to play the players in racquetball in Chicago all the time. I competed that way. I beat them most of the time. McMahon could beat me. He's too good for me. But most of them I could beat.

**Weeb Ewbank** hired me,[5] and we only had four coaches back in those days, so you had to do it all—you had to draft, you had to scout, you had to coach. You learned a lot under Weeb.

**He was** a great player.[6] He was a leader. He was the one who made it happen. Wore his

white shoes.

**I had** four brothers and two sisters. We were poor, but we didn't know it. We had clean clothes to wear and always had food on the table. We had great togetherness, really.

**I worked** digging ditches and building roads, all kinds of things, anything that paid.

**I got** the farm, 178 acres, and I lease about 420 acres. Bunch of cows and a bunch of horses.

**"46blitz" is** a horse of mine.

**I had** a bunch of tough players over the years. Wilber Marshall was a tough guy. Otis Wilson was a tough guy. Gerry Philbin was a tough guy with the Jets. Then I had Alan Page and Carl Eller and Jim Marshall. Jerome Brown was a super-tough guy. I told you before, we looked for brains and toughness. Dumb guys get you beat, and cowards get you beat.

**I don't** think there's anything misunderstood. You pretty well get what you see, don't you?

1. In the meeting with his defensive players the night before the Super Bowl.
2. Dan Hampton.
3. Gary Fencik.
4. William Perry.
5. As an assistant coach for the New York Jets, including the 1969 team that stunned the Baltimore Colts in Super Bowl III.
6. Jets quarterback Joe Namath.

# 1985 CHICAGO BEARS ROSTER

NFL CAREER: ● with Bears  ○ with other team (years shown below; parentheses = with other team)

| NO./PLAYER | POSITION | COLLEGE | HT. | WT. | NFL CAREER |
|---|---|---|---|---|---|
| 86 Anderson, Brad | Wide receiver | Arizona | 6-2 | 198 | 84 85 |
| 60 Andrews, Tom | Center | Louisville | 6-4 | 267 | 84 85 (87) |
| 84 Baschnagel, Brian | Wide receiver | Ohio State | 6-0 | 193 | 76 77 78 79 80 81 82 83 84 85 |
| 79 Becker, Kurt | Guard | Michigan | 6-5 | 280 | 82 83 84 85 86 87 88 (89) 90 |
| 62 Bortz, Mark | Guard | Iowa | 6-6 | 270 | 83 84 85 86 87 88 89 90 91 92 93 94 |
| 8 Buford, Maury | Punter | Texas Tech | 6-0 | 198 | (82 83 84) 85 86 (89 90 91) |
| 6 Butler, Kevin | Kicker | Georgia | 6-1 | 200 | 85 86 87 88 89 90 91 92 93 94 95 (96 97) |
| 54 Cabral, Brian | Linebacker | Colorado | 6-1 | 232 | (78 80) 81 82 83 84 85 86 |
| 74 Covert, Jim | Offensive tackle | Pittsburgh | 6-4 | 275 | 83 84 85 86 87 88 89 90 |
| 95 Dent, Richard | Defensive end | Tennessee State | 6-5 | 265 | 83 84 85 86 87 88 89 90 91 92 93 (94) 95 (96 97) |
| 22 Duerson, Dave | Safety | Notre Dame | 6-1 | 208 | 83 84 85 86 87 88 89 (90 91 92 93) |
| 88 Dunsmore, Pat | Tight end | Drake | 6-3 | 237 | 83 84 85 |
| 45 Fencik, Gary | Safety | Yale | 6-1 | 193 | 76 77 78 79 80 81 82 83 84 85 86 87 |
| 24 Fisher, Jeff | Defensive back | Southern California | 5-11 | 195 | 81 82 83 84 85 |
| 21 Frazier, Leslie | Cornerback | Alcorn State | 6-0 | 187 | 81 82 83 84 85 |
| 71 Frederick, Andy | Offensive tackle | New Mexico | 6-6 | 265 | (77 78 79 80 81 82) 83 84 85 |
| 4 Fuller, Steve | Quarterback | Clemson | 6-4 | 195 | (79 80 81 82 83) 84 85 86 |
| 83 Gault, Willie | Wide receiver | Tennessee | 6-0 | 180 | 83 84 85 86 87 (88 89 90 91 92 93) |
| 23 Gayle, Shaun | Defensive back | Ohio State | 5-11 | 193 | 84 85 86 87 88 89 90 91 92 93 (94) |
| 29 Gentry, Dennis | Running back | Baylor | 5-8 | 186 | 82 83 84 85 86 87 88 89 90 91 92 |
| 99 Hampton, Dan | Defensive end | Arkansas | 6-5 | 270 | 79 80 81 82 83 84 85 86 87 88 89 90 |
| 73 Hartenstine, Mike | Defensive end | Penn State | 6-3 | 254 | 75 76 77 78 79 80 81 82 83 84 85 86 (87) |
| 63 Hilgenberg, Jay | Center | Iowa | 6-3 | 264 | 81 82 83 84 85 86 87 88 89 90 91 (92 93) |
| 75 Humphries, Stefan | Guard | Michigan | 6-3 | 268 | 84 85 86 (87 88) |
| 98 Keys, Tyrone | Defensive end | Mississippi State | 6-7 | 270 | 83 84 85 (86 87 88) |
| 89 Krenk, Mitch | Tight end | Nebraska | 6-2 | 233 | 84 85 |
| 81 Maness, James | Wide receiver | Texas Christian | 6-1 | 174 | 85 |
| 82 Margerum, Ken | Wide receiver | Stanford | 6-0 | 180 | 81 82 83 85 86 (87) |
| 58 Marshall, Wilber | Linebacker | Florida | 6-1 | 225 | 84 85 86 87 (88 89 90 91 92 93 94 95) |
| 85 McKinnon, Dennis | Wide receiver | Florida State | 6-1 | 185 | 83 84 85 87 88 89 (90) |
| 9 McMahon, Jim | Quarterback | Brigham Young | 6-1 | 190 | 82 83 84 85 86 87 88 (89 90 91 92 93 94 95 96) |
| 76 McMichael, Steve | Defensive tackle | Texas | 6-2 | 265 | (80) 81 82 83 84 85 86 87 88 89 90 91 92 93 (94) |
| 87 Moorehead, Emery | Tight end | Colorado | 6-2 | 230 | (77 78 79 80) 81 82 83 84 85 86 87 88 |
| 51 Morrissey, Jim | Linebacker | Michigan State | 6-3 | 220 | 85 86 87 88 89 90 91 92 (93) |
| 96 Ortego, Keith | Wide receiver | McNeese State | 6-0 | 180 | 85 86 87 |
| 34 Payton, Walter | Running back | Jackson State | 5-11 | 202 | 75 76 77 78 79 80 81 82 83 84 85 86 87 |
| 72 Perry, William | Defensive tackle | Clemson | 6-2 | 308 | 85 86 87 88 89 90 91 92 (93) 94 |
| 48 Phillips, Reggie | Cornerback | Southern Methodist | 5-10 | 170 | 85 86 87 (89) |
| 53 Rains, Dan | Linebacker | Cincinnati | 6-1 | 222 | 82 83 84 85 86 |
| 27 Richardson, Mike | Cornerback | Arizona State | 6-0 | 188 | 83 84 85 86 87 88 (89) |
| 59 Rivera, Ron | Linebacker | California | 6-3 | 239 | 84 85 86 87 88 89 90 91 92 |
| 20 Sanders, Thomas | Running back | Texas A&M | 5-11 | 203 | 85 86 87 88 89 (90 91) |
| 50 Singletary, Mike | Linebacker | Baylor | 6-0 | 228 | 81 82 83 84 85 86 87 88 89 90 91 92 |
| 26 Suhey, Matt | Fullback | Penn State | 5-11 | 216 | 80 81 82 83 84 85 86 87 88 89 |
| 31 Taylor, Ken | Defensive back | Oregon State | 6-1 | 186 | 85 86 |
| 57 Thayer, Tom | Guard | Notre Dame | 6-4 | 280 | 85 86 87 88 89 90 91 92 (93) |
| 33 Thomas, Calvin | Running back | Illinois | 5-11 | 245 | 82 83 84 85 86 87 (88) |
| 52 Thrift, Cliff | Linebacker | E. Central Oklahoma | 6-2 | 235 | (79 80 81 82 83 84) 85 86 |
| 18 Tomczak, Mike | Quarterback | Ohio State | 6-1 | 195 | 85 86 87 88 89 90 (91 92 93 94 95 96 97) |
| 78 Van Horne, Keith | Offensive tackle | Southern California | 6-7 | 280 | 81 82 83 84 85 86 87 88 89 90 91 92 93 |
| 70 Waechter, Henry | Defensive tackle | Nebraska | 6-5 | 275 | 82 (83) 84 85 86 (87) |
| 55 Wilson, Otis | Linebacker | Louisville | 6-2 | 232 | 80 81 82 83 84 85 86 87 (89) |
| 80 Wrightman, Tim | Tight end | UCLA | 6-3 | 235 | 85 86 |

| BOTTOM ROW | SECOND ROW | THIRD ROW | FOURTH ROW | FIFTH ROW | TOP ROW |
|---|---|---|---|---|---|
| Steve Fuller | Jerry Vainisi<br>GENERAL MANAGER | Bill McGrane<br>DIRECTOR OF<br>COMMUNICATIONS | Brian McCaskey<br>COMMUNITY<br>INVOLVEMENT | Fred Caito<br>TRAINER | Mike Ditka<br>HEAD COACH |
| Kevin Butler | Matt Suhey | Cliff Thrift | Andy Frederick | Willie Gault | Ted Plumb<br>RECEIVERS COACH |
| Maury Buford | Mike Richardson | Dan Rains | William Perry | Brian Baschnagel | Ed Hughes<br>OFFENSIVE COORDINATOR |
| Jim McMahon | Dennis Gentry | Brian Cabral | Mike Hartenstine | Dennis McKinnon | Dale Haupt<br>DEFENSIVE LINE COACH |
| Mike Tomczak | Ken Taylor | Otis Wilson | Jim Covert | Brad Anderson | Jim LaRue<br>DEFENSIVE<br>BACKFIELD COACH |
| Thomas Sanders | Calvin Thomas | Tom Thayer | Stefan Humphries | Emery Moorehead | Johnny Roland<br>RUNNING BACKS COACH |
| Leslie Frazier | Walter Payton | Wilber Marshall | Steve McMichael | Pat Dunsmore | Steve Kazor<br>SPECIAL TEAMS /<br>TIGHT ENDS COACH |
| Dave Duerson | Gary Fencik | Ron Rivera | Keith Van Horne | Mitch Krenk | Dick Stanfel<br>OFFENSIVE LINE COACH |
| Shaun Gayle | Reggie Phillips | Tom Andrews | Kurt Becker | Richard Dent | Buddy Ryan<br>DEFENSIVE COORDINATOR |
| Jeff Fisher | Mike Singletary | Mark Bortz | Tim Wrightman | Keith Ortego | Jim Dooley<br>RESEARCH AND<br>QUALITY CONTROL |
| | Jim Morrissey | Jay Hilgenberg | James Maness | Tyrone Keys | |
| | Michael McCaskey<br>PRESIDENT | Henry Waechter | Ken Margerum | Dan Hampton | |
| | | Ray Earley<br>EQUIPMENT MANAGER | Gary Haeger<br>EQUIPMENT MANAGER | Clyde Emrich<br>STRENGTH COACH | |

# REGULAR-SEASON STATISTICAL SUMMARY

## FINAL STANDINGS

| NFC EAST | W | L | T | PF | PA |
|---|---|---|---|---|---|
| Dallas Cowboys | 10 | 6 | 0 | 357 | 333 |
| New York Giants | 10 | 6 | 0 | 399 | 283 |
| Washington Redskins | 10 | 6 | 0 | 297 | 312 |
| Philadelphia Eagles | 7 | 9 | 0 | 286 | 310 |
| St. Louis Cardinals | 5 | 11 | 0 | 278 | 414 |

| NFC CENTRAL | W | L | T | PF | PA |
|---|---|---|---|---|---|
| BEARS | 15 | 1 | 0 | 456 | 198 |
| Green Bay Packers | 8 | 8 | 0 | 337 | 355 |
| Minnesota Vikings | 7 | 9 | 0 | 346 | 359 |
| Detroit Lions | 7 | 9 | 0 | 307 | 366 |
| Tampa Bay Buccaneers | 2 | 14 | 0 | 294 | 448 |

| NFC WEST | W | L | T | PF | PA |
|---|---|---|---|---|---|
| Los Angeles Rams | 11 | 5 | 0 | 340 | 277 |
| San Francisco 49ers | 10 | 6 | 0 | 411 | 263 |
| New Orleans Saints | 5 | 11 | 0 | 294 | 401 |
| Atlanta Falcons | 4 | 12 | 0 | 282 | 452 |

| AFC EAST | W | L | T | PF | PA |
|---|---|---|---|---|---|
| Miami Dolphins | 12 | 4 | 0 | 428 | 320 |
| New York Jets | 11 | 5 | 0 | 393 | 264 |
| New England Patriots | 11 | 5 | 0 | 362 | 290 |
| Indianapolis Colts | 5 | 11 | 0 | 320 | 386 |
| Buffalo Bills | 2 | 14 | 0 | 200 | 381 |

| AFC CENTRAL | W | L | T | PF | PA |
|---|---|---|---|---|---|
| Cleveland Browns | 8 | 8 | 0 | 287 | 294 |
| Pittsburgh Steelers | 7 | 9 | 0 | 379 | 355 |
| Cincinnati Bengals | 7 | 9 | 0 | 441 | 437 |
| Houston Oilers | 5 | 11 | 0 | 284 | 412 |

| AFC WEST | W | L | T | PF | PA |
|---|---|---|---|---|---|
| Los Angeles Raiders | 12 | 4 | 0 | 354 | 308 |
| Denver Broncos | 11 | 5 | 0 | 380 | 329 |
| San Diego Chargers | 8 | 8 | 0 | 467 | 435 |
| Seattle Seahawks | 8 | 8 | 0 | 349 | 303 |
| Kansas City Chiefs | 6 | 10 | 0 | 317 | 360 |

## SCORE BY QUARTERS

| | | | | | |
|---|---|---|---|---|---|
| BEARS | 67 | 144 | 123 | 122 | **456** |
| Opponents | 50 | 77 | 34 | 37 | **198** |

## TEAM STATS

| | CHI. | OPP. |
|---|---|---|
| Total first downs | 343 | 236 |
| By rushing | 176 | 74 |
| By passing | 145 | 141 |
| By penalty | 22 | 21 |
| Third downs made/att. | 85-219 | 61-205 |
| Fourth downs made/att. | 5-13 | 6-16 |
| Total net yards | 5,837 | 4,135 |
| Avg. per game | 364.8 | 258.4 |
| Total plays | 1,085 | 945 |
| Avg. per play | 5.4 | 4.4 |
| Net yards rushing | 2,761 | 1,319 |
| Avg. per game | 172.6 | 82.4 |
| Total rushes | 610 | 359 |
| Net yards passing | 3,076 | 2,816 |
| Avg. per game | 192.2 | 176.0 |
| Sacked/yds lost | 43-227 | 64-483 |
| Gross yds. passing | 3,303 | 3,299 |
| Comp./att. | 237-432 | 249-522 |
| Comp. pct. | 54.9 | 47.7 |
| Had intercepted | 16 | 34 |
| Punts/avg. | 69-41.6 | 90-40.4 |
| Net punting avg. | 35.1 | 33.5 |
| Penalties/yds. | 104-912 | 115-934 |
| Fumbles/lost | 24-15 | 30-20 |
| Touchdowns | 51 | 23 |
| By rushing | 27 | 6 |
| By passing | 17 | 16 |
| By return | 7 | 1 |

## ABBREVIATIONS

**TDR:** Rushing touchdowns
**TDP:** Receiving touchdowns
**TDRT:** Return touchdowns
**PAT:** Points after
**FG:** Field goals
**S:** Safeties
**PTS.:** Points scored
**TB:** Touchbacks
**IN 20:** Punts inside opp. 20

**BLK.:** Punts blocked
**ATT.:** Attempts
**AVG.:** Average
**COMP.:** Completed passes
**PCT.:** Completion percentage
**INT.:** Passes intercepted
**FC:** Fair catches

## INDIVIDUAL STATS

### SCORING

| | TDR | TDP | TDRT | PAT | FG | S | PTS. |
|---|---|---|---|---|---|---|---|
| Butler | 0 | 0 | 0 | 51-51 | 31-38 | 0 | 144 |
| Payton | 9 | 2 | 0 | 0-0 | 0-0 | 0 | 66 |
| McKinnon | 0 | 7 | 0 | 0-0 | 0-0 | 0 | 42 |
| Fuller | 5 | 0 | 0 | 0-0 | 0-0 | 0 | 30 |
| Thomas | 4 | 0 | 0 | 0-0 | 0-0 | 0 | 24 |
| McMahon | 3 | 1 | 0 | 0-0 | 0-0 | 0 | 24 |
| Perry | 2 | 1 | 0 | 0-0 | 0-0 | 0 | 18 |
| Gentry | 2 | 0 | 1 | 0-0 | 0-0 | 0 | 18 |
| Suhey | 1 | 1 | 0 | 0-0 | 0-0 | 0 | 12 |
| Margerum | 0 | 2 | 0 | 0-0 | 0-0 | 0 | 12 |
| Gault | 0 | 1 | 1 | 0-0 | 0-0 | 0 | 12 |
| Wilson | 0 | 0 | 1 | 0-0 | 0-0 | 1 | 8 |
| Sanders | 1 | 0 | 0 | 0-0 | 0-0 | 0 | 6 |
| Moorehead | 0 | 1 | 0 | 0-0 | 0-0 | 0 | 6 |
| Wrightman | 0 | 1 | 0 | 0-0 | 0-0 | 0 | 6 |
| Dent | 0 | 0 | 1 | 0-0 | 0-0 | 0 | 6 |
| Frazier | 0 | 0 | 1 | 0-0 | 0-0 | 0 | 6 |
| Rivera | 0 | 0 | 1 | 0-0 | 0-0 | 0 | 6 |
| Richardson | 0 | 0 | 1 | 0-0 | 0-0 | 0 | 6 |
| McMichael | 0 | 0 | 0 | 0-0 | 0-0 | 1 | 2 |
| Waechter | 0 | 0 | 0 | 0-0 | 0-0 | 1 | 2 |
| TOTALS | 27 | 17 | 7 | 51-51 | 31-38 | 3 | 456 |
| OPPONENTS | 6 | 16 | 1 | 22-23 | 12-19 | 1 | 198 |

### FIELD GOALS

| | 1-19 | 20-29 | 30-39 | 40-49 | 50+ | TOTAL |
|---|---|---|---|---|---|---|
| Butler | 2-2 | 13-13 | 13-14 | 3-6 | 0-3 | 31-38 |
| OPPONENTS | 1-1 | 2-3 | 5-6 | 3-5 | 1-4 | 12-19 |

### PUNTING

| | NO. | YARDS | AVG. | TB | IN. 20 | LONG | BLK. |
|---|---|---|---|---|---|---|---|
| Buford | 68 | 2,870 | 42.2 | 14 | 18 | 69 | 0 |
| Team | 1 | 0 | 0 | 0 | 0 | 0 | 1 |
| TOTALS | 69 | 2,870 | 41.6 | 14 | 18 | 69 | 1 |
| OPPONENTS | 90 | 3,639 | 40.4 | 6 | 11 | 75 | 1 |

### RUSHING

| | ATT. | YARDS | AVG. | LONG | TD |
|---|---|---|---|---|---|
| Payton | 324 | 1,551 | 4.8 | 40 | 9 |
| Suhey | 115 | 471 | 4.1 | 17 | 1 |
| McMahon | 47 | 252 | 5.4 | 19 | 3 |
| Gentry | 30 | 160 | 5.3 | 21 | 2 |
| Thomas | 31 | 125 | 4.0 | 17 | 4 |
| Sanders | 25 | 104 | 4.2 | 28 | 1 |
| Fuller | 24 | 77 | 3.2 | 19 | 5 |
| Gault | 5 | 18 | 3.6 | 11 | 0 |
| Perry | 5 | 7 | 1.4 | 2 | 2 |
| Tomczak | 2 | 3 | 1.5 | 3 | 0 |
| McKinnon | 1 | 0 | .0 | 0 | 0 |
| Margerum | 1 | -7 | -7.0 | -7.0 | 0 |
| TOTALS | 610 | 2,761 | 4.5 | 40 | 27 |
| OPPONENTS | 359 | 1,319 | 3.7 | 37 | 6 |

### PASSING

| | COMP. | ATT. | YARDS | PCT. | AVG. | TD | INT. | LONG | SACKED/YDS. | RATING |
|---|---|---|---|---|---|---|---|---|---|---|
| McMahon | 178 | 313 | 2,392 | 56.9 | 7.64 | 15 | 11 | 70 | 28-125 | 82.8 |
| Fuller | 53 | 107 | 777 | 49.5 | 7.26 | 1 | 5 | 69 | 17-102 | 57.0 |
| Payton | 3 | 5 | 96 | 60.0 | 19.20 | 1 | 0 | 50 | 0-0 | 143.8 |
| Tomczak | 2 | 6 | 33 | 33.3 | 5.50 | 0 | 0 | 24 | 0-0 | 52.8 |
| Buford | 1 | 1 | 5 | 100.0 | 5.0 | 0 | 0 | 5 | 0 | — |
| TOTALS | 237 | 432 | 3,303 | 54.9 | 7.65 | 17 | 16 | 70 | 43-227 | 77.3 |
| OPPONENTS | 249 | 522 | 3,299 | 47.7 | 6.32 | 16 | 34 | 90 | 64-483 | 51.4 |

### RECEIVING

| | NO. | YARDS | AVG. | LONG | TD |
|---|---|---|---|---|---|
| Gault | 33 | 704 | 21.3 | 70 | 1 |
| McKinnon | 31 | 555 | 17.9 | 48 | 7 |
| Payton | 49 | 483 | 9.9 | 65 | 2 |
| Moorehead | 35 | 481 | 13.7 | 25 | 1 |
| Wrightman | 24 | 407 | 17.0 | 49 | 1 |
| Suhey | 33 | 295 | 8.9 | 35 | 1 |
| Margerum | 17 | 190 | 11.2 | 20 | 2 |
| Gentry | 5 | 77 | 15.4 | 30 | 0 |
| Thomas | 5 | 45 | 9.0 | 15 | 0 |
| Maness | 1 | 34 | 34.0 | 34 | 0 |
| McMahon | 1 | 13 | 13.0 | 13 | 1 |
| Sanders | 1 | 9 | 9.0 | 9 | 0 |
| Anderson | 1 | 6 | 6.0 | 6 | 0 |
| Perry | 1 | 4 | 4.0 | 4 | 1 |
| Total | 237 | 3,303 | 13.9 | 70 | 17 |
| OPPONENTS | 249 | 3,299 | 13.2 | 90 | 16 |

### INTERCEPTIONS

| | NO. | YARDS | AVG. | LONG | TD |
|---|---|---|---|---|---|
| Frazier | 6 | 119 | 19.8 | 33 | 1 |
| Duerson | 5 | 58 | 11.6 | 37 | 0 |
| Fencik | 5 | 38 | 7.6 | 22 | 0 |
| Marshall | 5 | 27 | 5.4 | 14 | 0 |
| Richardson | 4 | 174 | 43.5 | 90 | 1 |
| Wilson | 3 | 35 | 11.7 | 23 | 1 |
| Taylor | 3 | 28 | 9.3 | 18 | 0 |
| Dent | 2 | 10 | 5.0 | 9 | 1 |
| Singletary | 1 | 23 | 23.0 | 23 | 0 |
| TOTALS | 34 | 512 | 15.1 | 90 | 4 |
| OPPONENTS | 16 | 99 | 2.2 | 43 | 1 |

### KICKOFF RETURNS

| | NO. | YARDS | AVG. | LONG | TD |
|---|---|---|---|---|---|
| Gault | 22 | 577 | 26.2 | 99 | 1 |
| Gentry | 18 | 466 | 25.9 | 94 | 1 |
| Taylor | 1 | 18 | 18.0 | 18 | 0 |
| McKinnon | 1 | 16 | 16.0 | 16 | 0 |
| Sanders | 1 | 10 | 10.0 | 10 | 0 |
| TOTALS | 43 | 1,089 | 25.3 | 99 | 2 |
| OPPONENTS | 78 | 1,827 | 23.4 | 58 | 0 |

### PUNT RETURNS

| | NO. | FC | YARDS | AVG. | LONG | TD |
|---|---|---|---|---|---|---|
| Taylor | 25 | 8 | 198 | 7.9 | 21 | 0 |
| Ortego | 17 | 2 | 158 | 9.3 | 23 | 0 |
| Duerson | 6 | 0 | 47 | 7.8 | 11 | 0 |
| McKinnon | 4 | 0 | 44 | 11.0 | 17 | 0 |
| Maness | 2 | 0 | 9 | 4.5 | 5 | 0 |
| Gentry | 0 | 0 | 47 | 0 | 47 | 0 |
| Total | 54 | 10 | 503 | 9.3 | 47 | 0 |
| OPPONENTS | 23 | 9 | 203 | 8.8 | 29 | 0 |

## GAME 1
### SEPT. 8 at SOLDIER FIELD

# 38 | 28
**BEARS** | **BUCCANEERS**

| | | | | | |
|---|---|---|---|---|---|
| TAMPA BAY | 14 | 14 | 0 | 0 | **28** |
| BEARS | 7 | 10 | 14 | 7 | **38** |

### FIRST QUARTER

**BUCS:** Magee 1 pass from DeBerg (Igwebuike kick), 7:06.

**BEARS:** McKinnon 21 pass from McMahon (Butler kick), 12:11.

**BUCS:** House 44 pass from DeBerg (Igwebuike kick), 12:33.

### SECOND QUARTER

**BUCS:** Bell 11 pass from DeBerg (Igwebuike kick), 3:29.

**BEARS:** McMahon 1 run (Butler kick), 6:51.

**BEARS:** Butler 38 FG, 12:25.

**BUCS:** Wilder 3 run (Igwebuike kick), 13:51.

### THIRD QUARTER

**BEARS:** Frazier 29 interception return (Butler kick), :22.

**BEARS:** Suhey 9 pass from McMahon (Butler kick), 14:33.

### FOURTH QUARTER

**BEARS:** McMahon 1 run (Butler kick), 2:28.

### TEAM STATS

| | T.B. | CHI. |
|---|---|---|
| First downs | 17 | 27 |
| Total net yards | 307 | 436 |
| Rushes-yards | 29-166 | 34-185 |
| Passing yards | 141 | 251 |
| Return yards | 21 | 55 |
| Comp-att-int | 13-21-2 | 23-34-1 |
| Sacked-yards | 2-19 | 3-23 |
| Punts-avg | 6-37 | 2-58 |
| Fumbles-lost | 0-0 | 2-2 |
| Penalties-yards | 12-80 | 8-78 |
| Time of possession | 26:41 | 33:19 |

### INDIVIDUAL STATS

RUSHING
**Bucs:** Wilder 27-166, DeBerg 2-0.
**Bears:** Payton 17-120, Suhey 8-27, McMahon 4-18, Thomas 3-12, Gentry 2-8.

PASSING
**Bucs:** DeBerg 13-21-2-160.
**Bears:** McMahon 23-34-1-274.

RECEIVING
**Bucs:** Bell 6-74, House 1-44, Carter 3-18, Giles 1-18, Wilder 1-5, Magee 1-1.
**Bears:** Gault 4-60, McKinnon 4-58, Payton 6-37, Thomas 3-32, Moorehead 2-31, Wrightman 1-27, Margerum 2-20, Suhey 1-9.

MISSED FIELD GOALS
**Bucs:** Igwebuike 39.
**Bears:** Butler 63, 45.

Attendance: 57,828

## GAME 2
### SEPT. 15 at SOLDIER FIELD

# 20 | 7
**BEARS** | **PATRIOTS**

| | | | | | |
|---|---|---|---|---|---|
| NEW ENGLAND | 0 | 0 | 0 | 7 | **7** |
| BEARS | 7 | 3 | 10 | 0 | **20** |

### FIRST QUARTER

**BEARS:** McKinnon 32 pass from McMahon (Butler kick), 3:03.

### SECOND QUARTER

**BEARS:** Butler 21 FG, 14:23.

### THIRD QUARTER

**BEARS:** Suhey 1 run (Butler kick), 10:44.

**BEARS:** Butler 28 FG, 13:38.

### FOURTH QUARTER

**PATRIOTS:** James 90 pass from Eason (Franklin kick), 5:57.

### TEAM STATS

| | N.E. | CHI. |
|---|---|---|
| First downs | 10 | 18 |
| Total net yards | 206 | 369 |
| Rushes-yards | 16-27 | 44-160 |
| Passing yards | 179 | 209 |
| Return yards | 116 | 157 |
| Comp-att-int | 15-35-3 | 13-23-1 |
| Sacked-yards | 6-55 | 3-23 |
| Punts-avg | 11-47 | 8-37 |
| Fumbles-lost | 1-1 | 1-1 |
| Penalties-yards | 8-70 | 2-10 |
| Time of possession | 22:35 | 37:25 |

### INDIVIDUAL STATS

RUSHING
**Patriots:** Collins 7-19, James 7-5, Weathers 2-3.
**Bears:** Payton 11-39, Sanders 10-37, Suhey 9-36, Thomas 5-22, Gentry 4-10, McMahon 3-8, Fuller 1-8, McKinnon 1-0.

PASSING
**Patriots:** Eason 15-35-3-234.
**Bears:** McMahon 13-21-1-232, Fuller 0-1-0-0, Payton 0-1-0-0.

RECEIVING
**Patriots:** James 1-90, Ramsey 5-51, Williams 3-46, Jones 2-26, Collins 3-16, Morgan 1-5.
**Bears:** Wrightman 2-74, McKinnon 5-73, Gault 1-43, Moorehead 2-25, Margerum 2-16, Payton 1-1.

MISSED FIELD GOALS
None.

Attendance: 60,533

## GAME 3
### SEPT. 19 at THE METRODOME

# 33 | 24
**BEARS** | **VIKINGS**

| | | | | | |
|---|---|---|---|---|---|
| BEARS | 3 | 3 | 24 | 3 | **33** |
| MINNESOTA | 3 | 7 | 7 | 7 | **24** |

### FIRST QUARTER

**BEARS:** Butler 24 FG, 8:36.

**VIKINGS:** Stenerud 25 FG, 14:49.

### SECOND QUARTER

**BEARS:** Butler 19 FG, 11:35.

**VIKINGS:** Carter 14 pass from Kramer (Stenerud kick), 14:13.

### THIRD QUARTER

**BEARS:** Butler 34 FG, 3:30.

**VIKINGS:** Jones 9 pass from Kramer (Stenerud kick), 7:28.

**BEARS:** Gault 70 pass from McMahon (Butler kick), 7:47.

**BEARS:** McKinnon 25 pass from McMahon (Butler kick), 9:35.

**BEARS:** McKinnon 43 pass from McMahon (Butler kick), 14:27.

### FOURTH QUARTER

**VIKINGS:** Carter 57 pass from Kramer (Stenerud kick), 5:41.

**BEARS:** Butler 31 FG, 9:25.

### TEAM STATS

| | CHI. | MINN. |
|---|---|---|
| First downs | 21 | 23 |
| Total net yards | 480 | 445 |
| Rushes-yards | 30-127 | 15-34 |
| Passing yards | 353 | 411 |
| Return yards | 193 | 182 |
| Comp-att-int | 21-33-1 | 28-55-3 |
| Sacked-yards | 1-7 | 4-25 |
| Punts-avg | 3-40 | 3-43 |
| Fumbles-lost | 0-0 | 3-2 |
| Penalties-yards | 10-66 | 6-45 |
| Time of possession | 31:44 | 28:16 |

### INDIVIDUAL STATS

RUSHING
**Bears:** Payton 15-62, Suhey 8-41, McMahon 4-18, Fuller 2-4, Thomas 1-2.
**Vikings:** Nelson 5-18, Anderson 7-10, Brown 1-6, Coleman 2-0.

PASSING
**Bears:** McMahon 8-15-0-236, Fuller 13-18-1-124.
**Vikings:** Kramer 28-55-3-436.

RECEIVING
**Bears:** Gault 6-146, McKinnon 4-133, Suhey 1-21, Margerum 2-19, Payton 5-17, Moorehead 1-13, Anderson 1-6, Wrightman 1-5.
**Vikings:** Carter 4-102, Rhymes 3-89, Jordan 5-66, Lewis 4-66, Jones 4-43, Mularkey 2-26, Anderson 2-14, Rice 1-11, Nelson 2-10, Brown 1-9.

MISSED FIELD GOALS
**Bears:** Butler 34, 45.

Attendance: 61,242

## GAME 4
### SEPT. 29 at SOLDIER FIELD

# 45 | 10
**BEARS** | **REDSKINS**

| | | | | | |
|---|---|---|---|---|---|
| WASHINGTON | 7 | 3 | 0 | 0 | **10** |
| BEARS | 0 | 31 | 7 | 7 | **45** |

### FIRST QUARTER

**REDSKINS:** Riggins 7 run (Moseley kick), 8:52.

### SECOND QUARTER

**REDSKINS:** Moseley 32 FG, :06.

**BEARS:** Gault 99 kickoff return (Butler kick), :27.

**BEARS:** McKinnon 14 pass from McMahon (Butler kick), 2:33.

**BEARS:** Moorehead 10 pass from McMahon (Butler kick), 5:41.

**BEARS:** McMahon 13 pass from Payton (Butler kick), 10:33.

**BEARS:** Butler 28 FG, 14:56.

### THIRD QUARTER

**BEARS:** Payton 33 pass from McMahon (Butler kick), 9:37.

### FOURTH QUARTER

**BEARS:** Gentry 1 run (Butler kick), 9:33.

### TEAM STATS

| | WASH. | CHI. |
|---|---|---|
| First downs | 19 | 16 |
| Total net yards | 376 | 250 |
| Rushes-yards | 35-192 | 22-91 |
| Passing yards | 184 | 159 |
| Return yards | 182 | 217 |
| Comp-att-int | 21-39-2 | 14-21-1 |
| Sacked-yards | 4-25 | 3-14 |
| Punts-avg | 5-27 | 5-41 |
| Fumbles-lost | 1-1 | 0-0 |
| Penalties-yards | 10-85 | 6-50 |
| Time of possession | 34:25 | 25:35 |

### INDIVIDUAL STATS

RUSHING
**Redskins:** Rogers 13-80, Jenkins 2-39, Griffin 4-37, Riggins 11-29, Theismann 4-7, Wonsley 1-0.
**Bears:** McMahon 3-36, Sanders 3-35, Suhey 5-14, Payton 7-6, Thomas 1-1, Fuller 1-0, Gentry 2-(-1).

PASSING
**Redskins:** Theismann 21-39-2-209.
**Bears:** McMahon 13-19-1-160, Payton 1-1-0-13, Fuller 0-1-0-0.

RECEIVING
**Redskins:** Didier 8-92, Clark 5-76, Monk 4-14, Warren 1-12, Muhammed 1-8, Griffin 2-7.
**Bears:** McKinnon 3-50, Payton 2-41, Moorehead 3-34, Margerum 1-18, McMahon 1-13, Suhey 3-11, Thomas 1-6.

MISSED FIELD GOALS
None.

Attendance: 63,708

## GAME 5
### OCT. 6 at TAMPA STADIUM

# 27 | 19
**BEARS** | **BUCCANEERS**

| | | | | | |
|---|---|---|---|---|---|
| BEARS | 0 | 3 | 10 | 14 | **27** |
| TAMPA BAY | 0 | 12 | 0 | 7 | **19** |

### SECOND QUARTER

**BUCS:** Igwebuike 19 FG, 4:04.

**BUCS:** House 21 pass from DeBerg (kick failed), 8:38.

**BUCS:** Igwebuike 36 FG, 13:09.

**BEARS:** Butler 30 FG, 14:59.

### THIRD QUARTER

**BEARS:** McKinnon 21 pass from McMahon (Butler kick), 11:20.

**BEARS:** Butler 30 FG, 15:00.

### FOURTH QUARTER

**BEARS:** Payton 4 run (Butler kick), 7:09.

**BUCS:** Carter 25 pass from DeBerg (Igwebuike kick), 9:39.

**BEARS:** Payton 9 run (Butler kick), 14:08.

### TEAM STATS

| | CHI. | T.B. |
|---|---|---|
| First downs | 22 | 19 |
| Total net yards | 433 | 373 |
| Rushes-yards | 32-147 | 20-27 |
| Passing yards | 286 | 346 |
| Return yards | 156 | 134 |
| Comp-att-int | 22-34-2 | 23-43-2 |
| Sacked-yards | 1-6 | 0-0 |
| Punts-avg | 4-54 | 4-45 |
| Fumbles-lost | 2-1 | 3-1 |
| Penalties-yards | 9-67 | 5-40 |
| Time of possession | 32:09 | 27:51 |

### INDIVIDUAL STATS

RUSHING
**Bears:** Payton 16-63, McMahon 8-46, Suhey 6-38, Thomas 1-3, Gault 1-(-3).
**Bucs:** Wilder 18-29, DeBerg 1-0, Springs 1-(-2).

PASSING
**Bears:** McMahon 22-34-2-292.
**Bucs:** DeBerg 23-43-2-346.

RECEIVING
**Bears:** Moorehead 8-114, McKinnon 4-67, Gault 2-56, Suhey 5-30, Payton 1-9, Margerum 1-9, Thomas 1-7.
**Bucs:** Giles 7-112, House 6-100, Bell 3-50, Carter 2-46, Wilder 4-31, Magee 1-7.

MISSED FIELD GOALS
**Bucs:** Igwebuike 46.

Attendance: 51,795

## GAME 6
### OCT. 13 at CANDLESTICK PARK

**26** BEARS — **10** 49ERS

| | | | | | |
|---|---|---|---|---|---|
| BEARS | 13 | 3 | 0 | 10 | **26** |
| SAN FRANCISCO | 0 | 10 | 0 | 0 | **10** |

#### FIRST QUARTER

**BEARS:** Payton 3 run (Butler kick), 2:29.
**BEARS:** Butler 34 FG, 7:42.
**BEARS:** Butler 38 FG, 10:06.

#### SECOND QUARTER

**BEARS:** Butler 27 FG, 1:05.
**49ERS:** Williamson 43 interception return (Wersching kick), 6:03.
**49ERS:** Wersching 32 FG, 14:11.

#### FOURTH QUARTER

**BEARS:** Butler 29 FG, 1:51.
**BEARS:** Payton 17 run (Butler kick), 11:19.

### TEAM STATS

| | CHI. | S.F. |
|---|---|---|
| First downs | 22 | 11 |
| Total net yards | 372 | 183 |
| Rushes-yards | 39-189 | 12-67 |
| Passing yards | 183 | 116 |
| Return yards | 101 | 218 |
| Comp-att-int | 18-31-1 | 17-29-0 |
| Sacked-yards | 1-3 | 7-44 |
| Punts-avg | 3-45 | 7-48 |
| Fumbles-lost | 1-0 | 4-2 |
| Penalties-yards | 7-45 | 13-94 |
| Time of possession | 36:37 | 23:23 |

### INDIVIDUAL STATS

RUSHING
**Bears:** Payton 24-132, McMahon 4-24, Suhey 6-22, Gault 1-5, Perry 2-4, Gentry 1-3, Sanders 1-(-1).
**49ers:** Craig 4-42, Tyler 6-25, Montana 2-0.

PASSING
**Bears:** McMahon 18-31-1-186.
**49ers:** Montana 17-29-0-160.

RECEIVING
**Bears:** Wrightman 3-56, Gault 3-50, Payton 5-34, Suhey 5-25, Margerum 2-21.
**49ers:** Clark 4-41, Rice 3-37, Tyler 4-36, Ring 2-14, Craig 1-14, Francis 1-5.

MISSED FIELD GOALS
None.

**Attendance:** 60,523

---

## GAME 7
### OCT. 21 at SOLDIER FIELD

**23** BEARS — **7** PACKERS

| | | | | | |
|---|---|---|---|---|---|
| GREEN BAY | 7 | 0 | 0 | 0 | **7** |
| BEARS | 0 | 21 | 0 | 2 | **23** |

#### FIRST QUARTER

**PACKERS:** Lofton 27 pass from Dickey (Del Greco kick), 8:02.

#### SECOND QUARTER

**BEARS:** Payton 2 run (Butler kick), 1:19.
**BEARS:** Perry 1 run (Butler kick), 5:08.
**BEARS:** Payton 1 run (Butler kick), 13:49.

#### FOURTH QUARTER

**BEARS:** Safety, Wilson tackled Zorn in end zone, 10:59.

### TEAM STATS

| | G.B. | CHI. |
|---|---|---|
| First downs | 16 | 24 |
| Total net yards | 319 | 342 |
| Rushes-yards | 26-96 | 41-175 |
| Passing yards | 223 | 167 |
| Return yards | 64 | 131 |
| Comp-att-int | 14-31-4 | 15-32-0 |
| Sacked-yards | 4-27 | 3-5 |
| Punts-avg | 6-40 | 5-55 |
| Fumbles-lost | 2-1 | 7-4 |
| Penalties-yards | 10-70 | 6-45 |
| Time of possession | 24:25 | 35:35 |

### INDIVIDUAL STATS

RUSHING
**Packers:** Clark 14-50, Ivery 7-25, Ellis 3-10, Wright 1-8, Dickey 1-3.
**Bears:** Payton 25-112, Suhey 7-31, McMahon 4-27, Gentry 1-5, Perry 1-1, Tomczak 1-0, Fuller 2-(-1).

PASSING
**Packers:** Dickey 4-7-3-62, Wright 9-22-1-179, Zorn 1-2-0-9.
**Bears:** McMahon 12-26-0-144, Fuller 2-5-0-23, Buford 1-1-0-5.

RECEIVING
**Packers:** Lofton 7-103, Epps 3-59, Coffman 2-52, Clark 1-27, Ivery 1-9.
**Bears:** Payton 4-41, McKinnon 3-40, Suhey 3-33, Moorehead 2-28, Gault 2-18, Wrightman 1-12.

MISSED FIELD GOALS
None.

**Attendance:** 65,095

---

## GAME 8
### OCT. 27 at SOLDIER FIELD

**27** BEARS — **9** VIKINGS

| | | | | | |
|---|---|---|---|---|---|
| MINNESOTA | 0 | 7 | 0 | 2 | **9** |
| BEARS | 10 | 3 | 7 | 7 | **27** |

#### FIRST QUARTER

**BEARS:** McKinnon 33 pass from McMahon (Butler kick), 3:31.
**BEARS:** Butler 40 FG, 12:20.

#### SECOND QUARTER

**VIKINGS:** Nelson 1 run (Stenerud kick), :51.
**BEARS:** Butler 29 FG, 14:58.

#### THIRD QUARTER

**BEARS:** Wilson 23 interception return (Butler kick), 3:40.

#### FOURTH QUARTER

**BEARS:** Payton 20 pass from McMahon (Butler kick), 5:24.
**VIKINGS:** Safety, Elshire tackled Fuller in end zone, 7:15.

### TEAM STATS

| | MINN. | CHI. |
|---|---|---|
| First downs | 16 | 24 |
| Total net yards | 236 | 413 |
| Rushes-yards | 14-30 | 39-202 |
| Passing yards | 206 | 211 |
| Return yards | 137 | 132 |
| Comp-att-int | 21-46-5 | 19-34-1 |
| Sacked-yards | 4-30 | 1-4 |
| Punts-avg | 6-42 | 4-47 |
| Fumbles-lost | 0-0 | 1-1 |
| Penalties-yards | 8-60 | 6-77 |
| Time of possession | 25:18 | 34:42 |

### INDIVIDUAL STATS

RUSHING
**Vikings:** Nelson 8-22, Anderson 4-8, Rice 1-1, Kramer 1-(-1).
**Bears:** Payton 19-118, Suhey 10-34, Gentry 4-31, Sanders 4-6, McMahon 1-8, Gault 1-5.

PASSING
**Vikings:** Kramer 16-33-3-176, Wilson 5-13-2-60.
**Bears:** McMahon 18-31-1-181, Fuller 1-3-0-34.

RECEIVING
**Vikings:** Lewis 4-79, Nelson 5-44, Jordan 5-35, Carter 2-32, Anderson 3-21, Jones 1-13, Mularkey 1-12.
**Bears:** Moorehead 4-53, Suhey 5-38, Payton 5-37, Maness 1-34, McKinnon 1-33, Wrightman 2-13, Gault 1-7.

MISSED FIELD GOALS
None.

**Attendance:** 63,815

---

## GAME 9
### NOV. 3 at LAMBEAU FIELD

**16** BEARS — **10** PACKERS

| | | | | | |
|---|---|---|---|---|---|
| BEARS | 0 | 7 | 0 | 9 | **16** |
| GREEN BAY | 3 | 0 | 7 | 0 | **10** |

#### FIRST QUARTER

**PACKERS:** Del Greco 40 FG, 2:21.

#### SECOND QUARTER

**BEARS:** Perry 4 pass from McMahon (Butler kick), 14:35.

#### THIRD QUARTER

**PACKERS:** Clark 55 pass from Zorn (Del Greco kick), 9:45.

#### FOURTH QUARTER

**BEARS:** Safety, McMichael tackled Zorn in end zone, 2:42.
**BEARS:** Payton 27 run (Butler kick), 4:29.

### TEAM STATS

| | CHI. | G.B. |
|---|---|---|
| First downs | 16 | 15 |
| Total net yards | 253 | 242 |
| Rushes-yards | 37-188 | 28-87 |
| Passing yards | 65 | 155 |
| Return yards | 112 | 70 |
| Comp-att-int | 9-20-0 | 11-26-1 |
| Sacked-yards | 3-26 | 3-24 |
| Punts-avg | 8-39 | 6-37 |
| Fumbles-lost | 1-1 | 2-0 |
| Penalties-yards | 7-70 | 8-66 |
| Time of possession | 30:57 | 29:03 |

### INDIVIDUAL STATS

RUSHING
**Bears:** Payton 28-192, Suhey 4-6, Gault 1-0, McMahon 4-(-10).
**Packers:** Clark 17-58, Ivery 9-26, Lofton 1-3, Zorn 1-0.

PASSING
**Bears:** McMahon 9-20-0-91.
**Packers:** Zorn 11-26-1-179.

RECEIVING
**Bears:** Wrightman 2-29, Moorehead 1-21, Suhey 1-16, Payton 3-14, McKinnon 1-7, Perry 1-4.
**Packers:** Clark 3-62, Coffman 3-48, Epps 2-38, Ivery 2-22, Lofton 1-9.

MISSED FIELD GOALS
None.

**Attendance:** 55,343

---

## GAME 10
### NOV. 10 at SOLDIER FIELD

**24** BEARS — **3** LIONS

| | | | | | |
|---|---|---|---|---|---|
| DETROIT | 0 | 0 | 3 | 0 | **3** |
| BEARS | 7 | 7 | 7 | 3 | **24** |

#### FIRST QUARTER

**BEARS:** Fuller 1 run (Butler kick), 14:20.

#### SECOND QUARTER

**BEARS:** Thomas 7 run (Butler kick), 11:50.

#### THIRD QUARTER

**LIONS:** Murray 34 FG, 9:59.
**BEARS:** Fuller 5 run (Butler kick), 14:32.

#### FOURTH QUARTER

**BEARS:** Butler 39 FG, 9:18.

### TEAM STATS

| | DET. | CHI. |
|---|---|---|
| First downs | 8 | 26 |
| Total net yards | 106 | 360 |
| Rushes-yards | 22-68 | 55-250 |
| Passing yards | 38 | 110 |
| Return yards | 80 | 35 |
| Comp-att-int | 8-17-2 | 7-13-0 |
| Sacked-yards | 4-35 | 1-2 |
| Punts-avg | 3-31 | 2-21 |
| Fumbles-lost | 3-2 | 3-2 |
| Penalties-yards | 6-31 | 5-40 |
| Time of possession | 18:58 | 41:02 |

### INDIVIDUAL STATS

RUSHING
**Lions:** Jones 19-68, Moore 1-2, Hipple 2-(-2).
**Bears:** Payton 26-107, Suhey 16-102, Thomas 4-13, Gentry 2-13, Fuller 5-11, Gault 1-11, Margerum 1-(-7).

PASSING
**Lions:** Hipple 8-17-2-73.
**Bears:** Fuller 7-13-0-112, Tomczak 0-0-0-0.

RECEIVING
**Lions:** Mandley 2-20, Rubick 1-16, Nichols 2-14, Moore 1-14, Jones 2-7.
**Bears:** Payton 4-69, Wrightman 1-23, Suhey 1-12, Margerum 1-8.

MISSED FIELD GOALS
Bears: Butler 43.

**Attendance:** 53,467

## GAME 11
### NOV. 17 at TEXAS STADIUM

**44** BEARS — **0** COWBOYS

| | | | | | |
|---|---|---|---|---|---|
| BEARS | 7 | 17 | 3 | 17 | **44** |
| DALLAS | 0 | 0 | 0 | 0 | **0** |

#### FIRST QUARTER
**BEARS:** Dent 1 interception return (Butler kick), 13:12.

#### SECOND QUARTER
**BEARS:** Butler 44 FG, 5:13.
**BEARS:** Richardson 36 interception return (Butler kick), 9:19.
**BEARS:** Fuller 1 run (Butler kick), 12:02.

#### THIRD QUARTER
**BEARS:** Butler 46 FG, 14:24.

#### FOURTH QUARTER
**BEARS:** Butler 22 FG, 3:02.
**BEARS:** Thomas 17 run (Butler kick), 7:13.
**BEARS:** Gentry 16 run (Butler kick), 12:22.

### TEAM STATS

| | CHI. | DAL. |
|---|---|---|
| First downs | 18 | 12 |
| Total net yards | 378 | 171 |
| Rushes-yards | 40-216 | 16-52 |
| Passing yards | 162 | 119 |
| Return yards | 137 | 196 |
| Comp-att-int | 10-25-1 | 15-39-4 |
| Sacked-yards | 4-35 | 6-48 |
| Punts-avg | 6-44 | 10-38 |
| Fumbles-lost | 1-0 | 1-1 |
| Penalties-yards | 8-105 | 6-65 |
| Time of possession | 35:18 | 24:42 |

### INDIVIDUAL STATS

RUSHING
**Bears:** Payton 22-132, Gentry 3-24, Fuller 4-21, Thomas 4-19, Suhey 4-11, Sanders 2-8, Perry 1-1.
**Cowboys:** Dorsett 12-44, Hogeboom 1-8, Lavette 3-0.

PASSING
**Bears:** Fuller 9-24-1-164, Payton 1-1-0-33, Tomczak 0-0-0-0.
**Cowboys:** White 9-17-1-107, Hogeboom 6-22-3-60.

RECEIVING
**Bears:** Wrightman 2-61, Suhey 2-46, Gault 2-24, McKinnon 1-24, Gentry 1-22, Moorehead 1-16, Payton 1-4.
**Cowboys:** Renfro 3-45, Cornwell 1-32, Newsome 3-25, Cosbie 2-25, Hill 2-15, Dorsett 2-12, Fowler 1-9, Gonzalez 1-4.

MISSED FIELD GOALS
None.

**Attendance:** 63,855

## GAME 12
### NOV. 24 at SOLDIER FIELD

**36** BEARS — **0** FALCONS

| | | | | | |
|---|---|---|---|---|---|
| ATLANTA | 0 | 0 | 0 | 0 | **0** |
| BEARS | 0 | 20 | 7 | 9 | **36** |

#### SECOND QUARTER
**BEARS:** Butler 35 FG, :47.
**BEARS:** Butler 32 FG, 6:22.
**BEARS:** Payton 40 run (Butler kick), 8:52.
**BEARS:** Perry 1 run (Butler kick), 13:04.

#### THIRD QUARTER
**BEARS:** Thomas 2 run (Butler kick), 5:41.

#### FOURTH QUARTER
**BEARS:** Safety, Waechter tackled Holly in end zone, 1:46.
**BEARS:** Sanders 1 run (Butler kick), 11:25.

### TEAM STATS

| | ATL. | CHI. |
|---|---|---|
| First downs | 10 | 24 |
| Total net yards | 119 | 379 |
| Rushes-yards | 37-141 | 43-196 |
| Passing yards | (-22) | 183 |
| Return yards | 105 | 112 |
| Comp-att-int | 3-17-2 | 12-24-0 |
| Sacked-yards | 5-38 | 1-1 |
| Punts-avg | 7-38 | 4-38 |
| Fumbles-lost | 1-1 | 1-1 |
| Penalties-yards | 9-82 | 5-45 |
| Time of possession | 27:08 | 32:52 |

### INDIVIDUAL STATS

RUSHING
**Falcons:** Riggs 30-110, Archer 3-19, Washington 3-12, Austin 1-0.
**Bears:** Payton 20-102, Thomas 6-26, Sanders 5-19, Gentry 6-30, Fuller 2-11, Suhey 2-4, Tomczak 1-3, Perry 1-1.

PASSING
**Falcons:** Archer 2-15-2-10, Holly 1-2-0-6.
**Bears:** Fuller 10-20-0-151, Tomczak 2-4-0-33.

RECEIVING
**Falcons:** Cox 2-16, Riggs 1-1.
**Bears:** Gault 2-70, Wrightman 3-40, Moorehead 2-39, Payton 3-20, Sanders 1-9, McKinnon 1-6.

MISSED FIELD GOALS
None.

**Attendance:** 61,769

## GAME 13
### DEC. 2 at THE ORANGE BOWL

**38** DOLPHINS — **24** BEARS

| | | | | | |
|---|---|---|---|---|---|
| BEARS | 7 | 3 | 14 | 0 | **24** |
| MIAMI | 10 | 21 | 7 | 0 | **38** |

#### FIRST QUARTER
**DOLPHINS:** Moore 33 pass from Marino (Reveiz kick), 3:51.
**BEARS:** Fuller 1 run (Butler kick), 6:39.
**DOLPHINS:** Reveiz 47 FG, 9:04.

#### SECOND QUARTER
**DOLPHINS:** Davenport 1 run (Reveiz kick), :07.
**BEARS:** Butler 30 FG, 8:20.
**DOLPHINS:** Davenport 1 run (Reveiz kick), 13:03.
**DOLPHINS:** Moore 6 pass from Marino (Reveiz kick), 13:43.

#### THIRD QUARTER
**BEARS:** Fuller 1 run (Butler kick), 5:35.
**DOLPHINS:** Clayton 42 pass from Marino (Reveiz kick), 6:27.
**BEARS:** Margerum 19 pass from Fuller (Butler kick), 8:35.

### TEAM STATS

| | CHI. | MIA. |
|---|---|---|
| First downs | 23 | 17 |
| Total net yards | 343 | 335 |
| Rushes-yards | 37-167 | 24-90 |
| Passing yards | 176 | 245 |
| Return yards | 153 | 101 |
| Comp-att-int | 14-28-3 | 14-27-1 |
| Sacked-yards | 6-35 | 3-25 |
| Punts-avg | 3-29 | 3-45 |
| Fumbles-lost | 1-1 | 2-1 |
| Penalties-yards | 7-65 | 6-61 |
| Time of possession | 34:08 | 25:52 |

### INDIVIDUAL STATS

RUSHING
**Bears:** Payton 23-121, Suhey 7-19, Fuller 6-19, McMahon 1-8.
**Dolphins:** Nathan 15-74, Bennett 5-12, Davenport 3-2, Hampton 1-2.

PASSING
**Bears:** Fuller 11-21-2-169, McMahon 3-6-1-42, Payton 0-1-0-0.
**Dolphins:** Marino 14-27-1-270.

RECEIVING
**Bears:** Gault 2-79, Margerum 4-61, Moorehead 4-33, Payton 2-16, Wrightman 1-12, Gentry 1-10.
**Dolphins:** Duper 5-107, Clayton 5-88, Moore 4-75.

MISSED FIELD GOALS
**Dolphins:** Reveiz 51.

**Attendance:** 75,594

## GAME 14
### DEC. 8 at SOLDIER FIELD

**17** BEARS — **10** COLTS

| | | | | | |
|---|---|---|---|---|---|
| INDIANAPOLIS | 0 | 3 | 0 | 7 | **10** |
| BEARS | 0 | 3 | 7 | 7 | **17** |

#### SECOND QUARTER
**BEARS:** Butler 20 FG, 3:57.
**COLTS:** Allegre 30 FG, 9:26.

#### THIRD QUARTER
**BEARS:** Payton 16 run (Butler kick), 13:07.

#### FOURTH QUARTER
**BEARS:** Thomas 3 run (Butler kick), 8:51.
**COLTS:** Capers 61 pass from Pagel (Allegre kick), 9:03.

### TEAM STATS

| | IND. | CHI. |
|---|---|---|
| First downs | 10 | 22 |
| Total net yards | 232 | 328 |
| Rushes-yards | 21-99 | 44-191 |
| Passing yards | 133 | 137 |
| Return yards | 117 | 93 |
| Comp-att-int | 10-24-0 | 11-23-0 |
| Sacked-yards | 1-10 | 3-8 |
| Punts-avg | 4-50 | 4-44 |
| Fumbles-lost | 0-0 | 0-0 |
| Penalties-yards | 3-25 | 5-45 |
| Time of possession | 21:05 | 38:55 |

### INDIVIDUAL STATS

RUSHING
**Colts:** McMillan 13-61, Wonsley 7-42, Capers 1-(-4).
**Bears:** Payton 26-111, Suhey 8-17, McMahon 5-36, Thomas 5-27.

PASSING
**Colts:** Pagel 10-24-0-143.
**Bears:** McMahon 11-23-0-145.

RECEIVING
**Colts:** Capers 1-61, Beach 3-35, Bouza 2-16, Bentley 1-16, Williams 1-10, McMillan 1-3, Boyer 1-2.
**Bears:** Gentry 2-38, Gault 3-36, Moorehead 1-24, Payton 2-23, Suhey 2-17, Margerum 1-7.

MISSED FIELD GOALS
**Colts:** Allegre 25, 55.

**Attendance:** 59,997

## GAME 15
### DEC. 14 at GIANTS STADIUM

**19** BEARS — **6** JETS

| | | | | | |
|---|---|---|---|---|---|
| BEARS | 3 | 7 | 3 | 6 | **19** |
| NEW YORK | 3 | 0 | 3 | 0 | **6** |

#### FIRST QUARTER
**BEARS:** Butler 18 FG, 10:55.
**JETS:** Leahy 23 FG, 13:19.

#### SECOND QUARTER
**BEARS:** Wrightman 7 pass from McMahon (Butler kick), 4:02.

#### THIRD QUARTER
**JETS:** Leahy 55 FG, 1:57.
**BEARS:** Butler 31 FG, 4:06.

#### FOURTH QUARTER
**BEARS:** Butler 36 FG, 11:19.
**BEARS:** Butler 21 FG, 14:43.

### TEAM STATS

| | CHI. | N.Y. |
|---|---|---|
| First downs | 20 | 11 |
| Total net yards | 319 | 159 |
| Rushes-yards | 40-116 | 23-70 |
| Passing yards | 203 | 89 |
| Return yards | 36 | 106 |
| Comp-att-int | 15-31-1 | 12-26-0 |
| Sacked-yards | 5-12 | 4-33 |
| Punts-avg | 7-36 | 6-37 |
| Fumbles-lost | 1-0 | 3-3 |
| Penalties-yards | 5-46 | 5-45 |
| Time of possession | 39:36 | 20:24 |

### INDIVIDUAL STATS

RUSHING
**Bears:** Payton 28-53, Suhey 7-23, Gentry 2-22, McMahon 3-18.
**Jets:** McNeil 20-63, Hector 2-5, Paige 1-2.

PASSING
**Bears:** McMahon 15-31-1-215.
**Jets:** O'Brien 12-26-0-122.

RECEIVING
**Bears:** Payton 1-65, Gault 3-46, Wrightman 4-37, McKinnon 3-27, Moorehead 2-17, Suhey 1-16, Gentry 1-7.
**Jets:** McNeil 3-42, Shuler 3-29, Toon 3-20, Walker 1-11, Klever 1-11, Hector 1-9.

MISSED FIELD GOALS
None.

**Attendance:** 74,752

## GAME 16
DEC. 22 at PONTIAC SILVERDOME

**37** BEARS | **17** LIONS

| | | | | | |
|---|---|---|---|---|---|
| BEARS | 3 | 3 | 10 | 21 | **37** |
| DETROIT | 3 | 0 | 7 | 7 | **17** |

### FIRST QUARTER
**BEARS:** Butler 25 FG, 5:40.
**LIONS:** Murray 42 FG, 14:41.

### SECOND QUARTER
**BEARS:** Butler 24 FG, 13:03.

### THIRD QUARTER
**BEARS:** Gentry 94 kickoff return (Butler kick), :20.
**BEARS:** Butler 21 FG, 10:33.
**LIONS:** Lewis 2 pass from Hipple (Murray kick), 13:32.

### FOURTH QUARTER
**BEARS:** McMahon 14 run (Butler kick), 1:16.
**BEARS:** Rivera 5 fumble recovery return (Butler kick), 1:44.
**LIONS:** Jones 2 run (Murray kick), 3:59.
**BEARS:** Margerum 11 pass from McMahon (Butler kick), 13:00.

### TEAM STATS

| | CHI. | DET. |
|---|---|---|
| First downs | 20 | 22 |
| Total net yards | 382 | 326 |
| Rushes-yards | 33-161 | 21-73 |
| Passing yards | 221 | 253 |
| Return yards | 282 | 202 |
| Comp-att-int | 14-26-3 | 24-47-3 |
| Sacked-yards | 4-23 | 6-45 |
| Punts-avg | 1-40 | 3-41 |
| Fumbles-lost | 2-1 | 4-4 |
| Penalties-yards | 8-58 | 2-15 |
| Time of possession | 33:00 | 27:00 |

### INDIVIDUAL STATS

RUSHING
**Bears:** Payton 17-81, Suhey 8-46, McMahon 3-15, Gentry 3-15, Fuller 1-4, Thomas 1-0.
**Lions:** Jones 16-74, Moore 5-(-1).

PASSING
**Bears:** McMahon 13-22-2-194, Payton 1-1-0-50, Tomczak 0-2-0-0, Fuller 0-1-1-0.
**Lions:** Hipple 22-44-3-287, Ferguson 2-3-0-11.

RECEIVING
**Bears:** Payton 4-55, Gault 1-50, Wrightman 2-37, McKinnon 1-37, Moorehead 2-33, Suhey 3-21, Margerum 1-11.
**Lions:** Mandley 5-127, Thompson 9-101, Bland 5-48, Lewis 3-14, Moore 1-7, Jones 1-1.

MISSED FIELD GOALS
**Bears:** Butler 51.
**Lions:** Murray 55.

Attendance: 74,042

## GAME 17 • NFC SEMIFINAL GAME
JAN. 5 at SOLDIER FIELD

 **21** BEARS | **0** GIANTS

| | | | | | |
|---|---|---|---|---|---|
| NEW YORK | 0 | 0 | 0 | 0 | **0** |
| BEARS | 7 | 0 | 14 | 0 | **21** |

### FIRST QUARTER
**BEARS:** Gayle 5 punt return (Butler kick), 9:32.

### THIRD QUARTER
**BEARS:** McKinnon 23 pass from McMahon (Butler kick), 6:12.
**BEARS:** McKinnon 20 pass from McMahon (Butler kick), 14:23.

### TEAM STATS

| | N.Y. | CHI. |
|---|---|---|
| First downs | 10 | 17 |
| Total net yards | 181 | 363 |
| Rushes-yards | 14-32 | 44-147 |
| Passing yards | 149 | 216 |
| Return yards | 104 | 48 |
| Comp-att-int | 14-35-0 | 11-21-0 |
| Sacked-yards | 6-60 | 0-0 |
| Punts-avg | 9-38 | 6-37 |
| Fumbles-lost | 3-1 | 0-0 |
| Penalties-yards | 4-25 | 2-20 |
| Time of possession | 22:46 | 37:14 |

### INDIVIDUAL STATS

RUSHING
**Giants:** Morris 12-32, Galbreath 1-9, Williams 1-(-9).
**Bears:** Payton 27-93, Suhey 6-33, McMahon 5-18, Thomas 4-11, Gentry 1-(-1), McKinnon 1-(-7).

PASSING
**Giants:** Simms 14-35-0-209.
**Bears:** McMahon 11-21-0-216.

RECEIVING
**Giants:** Adams 3-65, Bavaro 4-36, Williams 1-33, Carpenter 3-24, McConkey 1-23, Johnson 1-17, Galbreath 1-11.
**Bears:** Gault 3-68, McKinnon 3-52, Wrightman 1-46, Gentry 1-41, Suhey 2-5, Payton 1-4.

MISSED FIELD GOALS
**Giants:** Schubert 19.
**Bears:** Butler 26, 49, 38.

Attendance: 62,076

## GAME 18 • NFC CHAMPIONSHIP GAME
JAN. 12 at SOLDIER FIELD

 **24** BEARS | **0** RAMS

| | | | | | |
|---|---|---|---|---|---|
| LOS ANGELES | 0 | 0 | 0 | 0 | **0** |
| BEARS | 10 | 0 | 7 | 7 | **24** |

### FIRST QUARTER
**BEARS:** McMahon 16 run (Butler kick), 5:25.
**BEARS:** Butler 34 FG, 10:34.

### THIRD QUARTER
**BEARS:** Gault 22 pass from McMahon (Butler kick), 8:04.

### FOURTH QUARTER
**BEARS:** Marshall 52 fumble recovery return (Butler kick), 12:23.

### TEAM STATS

| | L.A. | CHI. |
|---|---|---|
| First downs | 13 | 9 |
| Total net yards | 130 | 232 |
| Rushes-yards | 26-86 | 33-91 |
| Passing yards | 44 | 141 |
| Return yards | 92 | 40 |
| Comp-att-int | 10-31-1 | 16-25-0 |
| Sacked-yards | 3-22 | 3-23 |
| Punts-avg | 11-39 | 10-36 |
| Fumbles-lost | 4-2 | 3-1 |
| Penalties-yards | 4-25 | 6-48 |
| Time of possession | 25:33 | 34:27 |

### INDIVIDUAL STATS

RUSHING
**Rams:** Dickerson 17-46, Redden 9-40.
**Bears:** Payton 18-32, McMahon 4-28, Suhey 6-23, Gentry 2-9, Thomas 3-(-1).

PASSING
**Rams:** Brock 10-31-1-66.
**Bears:** McMahon 16-25-0-164.

RECEIVING
**Rams:** Hunter 3-29, Brown 2-14, Dickerson 3-10, Duckworth 1-8, Ellard 1-5.
**Bears:** Gault 4-56, Payton 7-48, Moorehead 2-28, McKinnon 1-17, Wrightman 1-8, Suhey 1-7.

MISSED FIELD GOALS
None.

Attendance: 63,522

## GAME 19 • SUPER BOWL XX
### JAN. 26 at NEW ORLEANS SUPERDOME

  **46** **10**

BEARS      PATRIOTS

| | | | | | |
|---|---|---|---|---|---|
| **BEARS** | 13 | 10 | 21 | 2 | **46** |
| **NEW ENGLAND** | 3 | 0 | 0 | 7 | **10** |

#### FIRST QUARTER

**PATRIOTS:** Franklin 36 FG, 1:19.
**Drive:** 4 plays, 0 yards.
**Key play:** McGrew recovery of Payton fumble at Bears' 19.

**BEARS:** Butler 28 FG, 5:40.
**Drive:** 8 plays, 59 yards.
**Key play:** Gault 43 pass from McMahon.

**BEARS:** Butler 24 FG, 13:39.
**Drive:** 7 plays, 7 yards.
**Key play:** Hampton recovery of Eason fumble at New England 13.

**BEARS:** Suhey 11 run (Butler kick), 14:37.
**Drive:** 2 plays, 13 yards.
**Key play:** Singletary recovery of James fumble at New England 13.

#### SECOND QUARTER

**BEARS:** McMahon 2 run (Butler kick), 7:36.
**Drive:** 10 plays, 59 yards.
**Key play:** Suhey 24 pass from McMahon.

**BEARS:** Butler 25 FG, 15:00.
**Drive:** 11 plays, 72 yards.
**Key play:** Margerum 29 pass from McMahon.

#### THIRD QUARTER

**BEARS:** McMahon 1 run (Butler kick), 7:38.
**Drive:** 9 plays, 96 yards.
**Key play:** Gault 60 pass from McMahon.

**BEARS:** Phillips 28 interception return (Butler kick), 8:44.

**BEARS:** Perry 1 run (Butler kick), 11:38.
**Drive:** 6 plays, 37 yards.
**Key play:** Marshall recovery of James fumble at 50, returned by Marshall and Wilson to 37.

#### FOURTH QUARTER

**PATRIOTS:** Fryar 8 pass from Grogan (Franklin kick), 1:46.
**Drive:** 15 plays, 76 yards.
**Key play:** Morgan 21 pass from Grogan.

**BEARS:** Safety, Waechter tackled Grogan in end zone, 9:24.

### TEAM STATS

| | CHI. | N.E. |
|---|---|---|
| First downs | 23 | 12 |
| By rushing | 13 | 1 |
| By passing | 9 | 10 |
| By penalty | 1 | 1 |
| Third-down conversions | 7-14 | 1-10 |
| Offensive plays | 76 | 54 |
| Total net yards | 408 | 123 |
| Yards per play | 5.4 | 2.3 |
| Rushes-yards | 49-167 | 11-7 |
| Gain per rush | 3.4 | 0.6 |
| Passing yards | 241 | 116 |
| Comp-att-int | 12-24-0 | 17-36-2 |
| Gain per pass | 10.0 | 3.2 |
| Sacked-yards | 3-15 | 7-61 |
| Return yards | 144 | 175 |
| Punt return yards | 2-20 | 2-22 |
| Kickoff return yards | 4-49 | 7-153 |
| Interceptions | 2-75 | 0-0 |
| Fumbles-lost | 3-2 | 4-4 |
| Punts-avg | 4-43 | 6-44 |
| Penalties-yards | 6-35 | 5-35 |
| Touchdowns | 5 | 1 |
| By rushing | 4 | 0 |
| By passing | 0 | 1 |
| By returns | 1 | 0 |
| Field goals | 3-3 | 1-1 |
| Time of possession | 39:15 | 20:45 |

**Attendance:** 73,818

### INDIVIDUAL STATS

RUSHING (No.-Yds.-Avg.-Long-TD)
**Bears:** Payton 22-61-2.8-7-0, Suhey 11-52-4.7-11-1, Gentry 3-15-5.0-8-0, Sanders 4-15-3.8-11-0, McMahon 5-18-2.8-7-2, Thomas 2-8-4.0-7-0, Perry 1-1-1.0-1-1, Fuller 1-1-1.0-1-0.
**Patriots:** Collins 3-4-1.3-3-0, Weathers 1-3-3.0-3-0, Grogan 1-3-3.0-3-0, James 5-1-0.2-3-0, Hawthorne 1-(-4)-(-4.0)-(-4)-0.

PASSING (Comp.-Att.-Yds.-Pct.-TD-Int.)
**Bears:** McMahon 12-20-256-.600-0-0, Fuller 0-4-0-.000-0-0.
**Patriots:** Eason 0-6-0-.000-0-0, Grogan 17-30-177-.567-1-2.

RECEIVING (No.-Yds.-Avg.-Long-TD)
**Bears:** Gault 4-129-32.3-60-0, Gentry 2-41-20.5-27-0, Margerum 2-36-18.0-29-0, Moorehead 2-22-11.0-14-0, Suhey 1-24-24.0-24-0, Thomas 1-4-4.0-4-0.
**Patriots:** Morgan 7-70-10.0-16-0, Starring 2-39-19.5-24-0, Fryar 2-24-12.0-16-1, Collins 2-19-9.5-11-0, Ramsey 2-16-8.0-11-0, James 1-6-6.0-6-0, Weathers 1-3-3.0-3-0.

INTERCEPTIONS
**Bears:** Phillips 1-28, Morrissey 1-47.
**Patriots:** None.

TACKLES-ASSISTS-SACKS
**Bears:** Phillips 7-0-0, Marshall 4-0-.5, Duerson 4-0-0, Hampton 2-1-1.5, Dent 2-1-1, Fencik 2-1-0, Rivera 2-0-0, Cabral 2-0-0, Wilson 1-1-1.5, Singletary 1-1-0, Richardson 1-1-0, Gayle 1-0-0, Taylor 1-0-0, Perry 1-0-0, Hartenstine 1-0-0, Ortego 1-0-0, McMichael 0-0-1.5, Waechter 0-0-1.
**Patriots:** Blackmon 7-1-0, Nelson 6-3-0, Marion 6-1-0, R. James 5-1-0, Tippett 5-1-0, Lippett 5-0-0, Owens 4-1-2, McGrew 3-3-0, Veris 3-2-0, Hawthorne 3-0-0, Thomas 2-1-1, Adams 2-1-0, McSwain 2-0-0, Clayborn 2-0-0, Rembert 2-0-0, Gibson 1-0-0, Ingram 1-0-0, Creswell 1-0-0, C. James 1-0-0, Morgan 1-0-0, Dawson 1-0-0.

PUNTING
**Bears:** Buford 4-43.3.
**Patriots:** Camarillo 6-43.8.

PUNT RETURNS
**Bears:** Ortego 2-20.
**Patriots:** Fryar 2-22.

KICKOFF RETURNS
**Bears:** Gault 4-49.
**Patriots:** Starring 7-153.

MISSED FIELD GOALS
None.

## CREDITS

### Chicago Tribune

**PUBLISHER** David Hiller

**EDITOR** Ann Marie Lipinski

**MANAGING EDITOR** James O'Shea

**DEPUTY MANAGING EDITOR, NEWS** George de Lama

# THE '85 BEARS
## STILL CHICAGO'S TEAM

**EDITORS** Dan McGrath, Bill Adee

**PHOTO EDITORS** John Konstantaras, José Moré

**ART DIRECTOR** Jason McKean

**COPY EDITORS** Tom Carkeek, Rich Strom

**IMAGING** Don Bierman, Kathy Celer, Min Pak, Jennifer Fletcher, Peggy Huber, Hung Vu, William Avorio, John Anderson, Christine Bruno

**STATISTICS** Steve Layton

The accounts in this book are based on the reporting of Don Pierson, John Mullin and Fred Mitchell.

**PROJECT MANAGERS** Bill Parker, Tony Majeri , Susan Zukrow

**PHOTO CREDITS**

Chuck Berman: 89 (bottom right)

Charles Cherney: vi-vii, viii, ix, x-xi, 12-13, 14-15, 16-17, 18 (left), 20-21, 22 (top left), 22 (bottom left), 26 (bottom), 28, 29, 30-31, 32-33, 40-41, 41 (top), 48-49, 52-53, 60-61, 64-65, 77 (top), 84-85, 91-119, 128

Chicago Tribune archives: 18 (top right), 18 (bottom right)

Anne Cusack: 23, back cover

Bob Fila: 34 (top left), 35 (bottom right), 36-37

Mitch Friedman/Chicago Bears: 121

Frank Hanes: 68 (bottom), 86, 87, 88 (bottom left), 88 (bottom right), 89 (bottom left)

Bill Hogan: 88-89 (top)

Bob Langer: ii-iii, iv-v, 19, 38, 39, 42-43, 44-45, 46 (top), 51 (right), 52 (left), 56, 57, 58 (left), 58-59, 62, 63, 64 (left), 66-67, 70-71, 73, 74-75, 76, 78-79, 81 (top), 81 (bottom), 82-83

Jerry Tomaselli: 47

Ed Wagner Jr.: front cover, 24-25, 26 (top left), 26-27, 34-35, 42 (left), 45 (right), 46 (bottom), 49 (top), 50, 51 (left), 54-55, 55 (right), 60 (left), 68 (top), 68-69, 72, 77 (bottom), 80-81

Chris Walker: i, 22 (top right)

# Walter Payton

## 1954-1999

**I'm gonna** close by saying life is short. It's oh, so sweet. … I'm happy to say that everyone that I've met in my life, I have gained something from them, be it negative or positive, it reinforced my life in some aspect …

**The fans** are what make this game. Without you being out here and coming to this Hall of Fame, it wouldn't be professional football. So I stand here and I applaud you for supporting and staying with the National Football League and these players here. Thank you.

*—At his acceptance speech to the Pro Football Hall of Fame in Canton, Ohio, Aug. 1, 1993*